Insanity or Epiphany Illusory

Insanity or Epiphany Illusory

An account of a journey of self-deception!

Andrew Michael Lawless

authorHOUSE®

AuthorHouse™
1663 Liberty Drive
Bloomington, IN 47403
www.authorhouse.com
Phone: 1-800-839-8640

Published by AuthorHouse   02/28/2013

ISBN: 978-1-4817-1869-1 (sc)
ISBN: 978-1-4817-2001-4 (e)

Library of Congress Control Number: 2013903440

Contents

Preface ix

Chapter 1   A Consideration 1
Chapter 2   Introduction 2
Chapter 3   Background 4
Chapter 4   An Open Mind 9
Chapter 5   The Training 12
Chapter 6   The Battle Begins 22
Chapter 7   Round Two, the Ego
                 Reasserts Itself 38
Chapter 8   Another Regrouping
                 and the Seeming Victory Thereof 52
Chapter 9   The Goose is on the Loose 66
Chapter 10   The Dark Night Goes
                 Completely Black, Nearly 72
Chapter 11   Good and Compliant Boy
                 Interrupted 78
Chapter 12   The First Rays of Dawn 81
Chapter 13   The Healing Begins 87
Chapter 14   Two Feet on the Ground 89
Chapter 15   A Glimpse into the Ultimate
                 Mind-fucker that is Me 95

Chapter 16 Warning! Don't try this
             at Home You Must be a Good and
             Well-trained Psycho.............................107
Chapter 17 File Reopened 109

Lyrics.. 111
Bibliographical References 135
Glossary.. 137

"What I do is not out of a want of respect for authority, but in adherence to a higher law"

-Mohandas Gandhi

"People say I'm crazy
Doing what I'm doing
Well they give me all kinds of warnings
To save me from ruin . . ."

-John Lennon

"I come as a thief in the night."
"Judge not ye brethren lest you be judged by the same measure."

-The Master

Masquerading as a man with a reason
My charade is the event of the season
And if I claim to be a wise man
It surly means that I don't know . . ."

-Kansas

"Be werry werry quiet . . . we're huntin' wabbit."

-Elmer Fudd

Preface

The succeeding chapters, in a deja vu moment, at the risk of initiating a pattern of redundancy, still do not assuage or render justice to the egomaniac to end all that I am, so, fasten your seatbelts while I endeavor to take you on a ride into the ultimate mind-fucker that I A.M, I'll start with the beginning of the end, or the middle, or maybe just 7/8th.

I come as a brother
Seems there be something in a name
On a quest to find truth
Even if I go insane
No life, no death
Not within this illusory game
I seek not in purport
I've no concern for personal gain . . .

Andrew Lawless

1
A Consideration

"you are the salt of the Earth." Thus spoke the
Master.
What the hell is that supposed to mean I often
thought.
And the only reasonable meaning I could derive
from it is thus: Take things with a grain of salt, as
the saying goes, and it is thus my suggestion upon
the reading of these "accounts."

"It is also my suggestion that you read this in its
entirety."
Bibliographical references and glossary inclusive
and upon completion re-read the introduction
before formulating an opinion.
It was written with a wry comedic twist, consider
it thusly.

2
Introduction

What follows in these writings is an account of my experiences, with the exception of some brief background focusing mainly from the time period of 1998 to present. It is not my intention to purport any sort of authoritative misguided stance of truth that beckons your adherence; rather it is that which is aptly titled, "A Journey of Self Deception." Make of it what you will, for in all honesty it is still my greatest struggle to decipher what if any meaning there was and is in all if not any of it. For the purpose of being concise, it will be a somewhat brief overview of these experiences and seeming occurrences and I refer to them as seeming intentionally as you will come to understand for yourself. For to go into them in exact perspective detail would require more time, paper and ink than any of us would care to indulge in. Prior to deciding to document these, my own experiences, I came to a preliminary decision, I would write this in a natural flowing manner, recounting that which I can all the while, putting my trust in God that what ensues will serve faithfully the purpose if any that it is intended for. I'm not under any *delusive pretense that this is of if any sort of import, as you will see for yourself I went that road. Rather I get the strange sense that this will be therapeutic and perhaps cautionary to those who seek higher or greater understanding from falling into the same mind traps I did. Insanity or Epiphany, I still don't know!*

3
Background

October 28, 1970 at 5:38 a.m., as they tell me for I don't remember it, I have to be honest, I can't very well verify it, I was born.

While I was raised Roman Catholic, the blaring contradictions in this dogmatic rigid school of thought were quite obvious to me even as a child. No we weren't exactly church going folks, but on the occasions we did attend, this to me had all the reeking of a big steaming pile of horse shit. Consequently I avoided it like the plague, even going so far as to fake being sick so I didn't have to go to CCD. When my youngest sister was born, the house we currently occupied in Islip, Long Island went from being too small to beyond ridiculous. I didn't know it yet but I actually hit pay dirt. We relocated to a bigger house in a part of Bay Shore that was still Islip Schools, thankfully not St Maria's Parish. When my parents went to register me for Confirmation, they were informed by the parish that they hadn't contributed enough money. When they petitioned the diocese they were told there would be no exceptions. Nuts! Ultimately that ended up being the end of my affiliation with said religion. It wasn't as if we were atheists or anything, my parents believed in God and imparted that unto us, but to coin a term I would hear some years later, "church isn't four walls."

Flash forward. It's the morning of September 25, 1982 I'm awakened from a deep sleep, lying in my living room, to the sounds of hysterical crying. There are policemen there and while this is not so much of an uncommon occurrence being my father is a police officer, they're not his guys. "What's going on here?" I wonder. My older sister rushes to me in a fit of hysteria, "Danny's dead Andrew," she cries out. I instantly burst into tears. My brother, the person who I'm closest to of anyone in the entire world, is gone. It was a horrible car accident and in its wake I'm left with a devastating most blunt tangible realization. "Nothing will ever be the same again!"

Flash forward two and a half years, my father is diagnosed with cancer. It's bad, terminal, the prognosis is that he doesn't have very much time. I watch a robustly stern man of strong character wither away to nothing and on the afternoon of 19, June 1985 I come home from playing softball to the sound of a faint weak voice calling my name for help. It's my father; he had collapsed on the floor of his bedroom. I react with the detached mindset of total shock; I call 911, then my mother. He's rushed to the hospital where after being administered last rites, we gather around his bed. "Hold his hand," my mother says to me "he can hear you." I know he can't, this is not my father anymore; I can't believe this is happening! He succumbs to his illness shortly after, later that afternoon and I'm left with the dawning of that awareness once again, "Nothing will ever be the same again!

In the years that follow a change occurs within me, I'm wild and reckless, I don't much care anymore. What does it matter if I live or die? No, I'm not suicidal, not from the point of conscious thought, I simply don't care if I Live or die. In these times I drink often, as would be a pattern that would repeat itself in years to come. I've got to dull this pain. I put up a good front though, for the sake of my mother and siblings and continue onward. Athletics, which I shared in most closely with my brother and then father, are no longer important to me. One by one I quit every sport that I enjoyed and showed promise in. They mean nothing to me now, very little does. June, 1988, I graduate high school, remarkably still with decent grades; of the colleges I'm accepted to I elect to attend the University of Hartford. I've decided to follow my brother's footsteps and study electrical engineering. They have an accredited engineering program, it seems a good fit. Upon attending the orientation for incoming freshmen I meet, befriend and agree to room with Jason Leonard. He plays guitar, I always wanted to learn how to play guitar, a seemingly inconsequential fascination that would change the course of my life and begin the process of mending. As aforementioned, it would begin the process, the realization of which would take some years to manifest. I play guitar day and night, totally obsessed with it, all the while neglecting my studies and at the conclusion of my junior year the funds run out. I've lost my scholarship, which requires a standard of academic achievement to retain, am wasting time and money and it's just not there to waste anymore. My mother and I decide I will not return there to graduate. I go to work to help with the household expenses and bills.

What ensues in the following years in hindsight is quite remarkable. I'm brought back from the brink of apathy through my love for music, most specifically the Blues. It provides me with an outlet for the pain in the form of constructive creative expression. I'm a natural, and am tearing up the guitar in local bars. Of all those whose influence I've come under, I'm drawn to Stevie Ray Vaughn and Jimi Hendrix. Their mystique fascinates me. Learning all I can about them I learn they were both very spiritual people in their own unique ways and forms of practice. It's a realization that would ultimately steer the course of my life more profoundly than any other. I begin reading Urantia, courtesy of Stevie's interest in it and go on to consume just about any form of literature pertaining to spirit, on a mission to become aware. Of that which I read Paramahansa Yogananda's autobiography of a Yogi Hit home. Upon completing it I immediately send for their home lessons in the practice of Kriya Yoga, a form of meditation that promises to deliver direct perceptible realization of God. I practice their techniques for approximately two and one half years. It's during this time that the major thrust of this account begins.

4
An Open Mind

I'm sitting on the couch in my room, getting stoned and playing guitar. I would like it this way for some years to come. I put my guitar down, put on the T.V. and begin aimlessly watching, surfing through the channels. I come across something that completely blows my mind, it's a show called The Other Side. On it is medium James Van Praague: he's relaying messages from apparently deceased people to those they're survived by. It occurs to me that even the concept of that thought beckons some sort of reconsideration. How does he know these things?

I thumb through Urantia, as previously stated, courtesy of reference to it in Stevie Ray Vaughn's autobiography. "This is really some crazy shit!" I think, how the hell does anybody know this, in the main thrust of the thought, but I read it. Not exactly a pleasurable read but if Stevie liked it I'll give it a shot. All the while I'm involved in it: my thoughts turn to my father and brother. When will I be with them again?

Onward and upward I go yet now with a twist. I start to adopt the concept of God as my father and all others as my brother. I know what you're going to say, any shrink worth his thirst to administer pharmaceuticals would have a field day with that one. A classic case of substitution, it's obvious to me, but I go with it, it seems innocent enough and strangely liberating. It seems to me that that's the basic premise of all I'm reading anyway and I've got an inside track on that one. I begin praying fervently, something I gave up on years prior, but in my prayers while I didn't know it yet. I'm employing a technique commonly referred to as visualization. I climb a mountain in my mind and begin to realize the presence of a crow each time. He leads me up the mountain where I encounter and am faced with Jesus. Jesus seems to be a pretty cool character in my mind. I tell him each time I'd like to be a successful musician, but not only that, I want to be like Hendrix and Stevie. Not exactly any sort of deep spiritual insight just yet, I'm more concerned with success and the likes. And so enters the first hint of revelatory fraud in my newly found spiritual perspective.

My cousin informs me she's going to a psychic fair. I think of that Van Praague guy and decide to go with her. I enlist my mom and sister, my cousin's brother's (obviously also my cousin) girlfriend is also on board and off we go into the fascinating possibility that is the Huntington Hilton. It is there that I meet the love of all my lives though it wasn't even so much as a blip of a suspicion just yet. She reads me. I make reference to Stevie and Jimi; I refer to them as friends, not as musicians or anything of any notoriety. She brings them through, I'm hooked. These seemingly loving down to earth people are privy to something I'm not; I've got to learn all I can about it. My cousin's girlfriend Maria, who also happened to become one of my closest friends and I decide to find out more. We look into any sort of classes we can find in spiritualism.

5
The Training

Maria and I find a woman who teaches
Shamanism we're psyched! We love nature,
fairies and the like, and are looking forward
to quenching our spiritual thirst. We begin, we
practice forms of meditation and divination,
which the instructor leads us through but mostly
seems like hocus pocus. Within me lies a deep love
for the Native American belief system but this
was not such a good representation of said beliefs.
It was then that the first evidence of realization
dawned on me. Be very wary of those who claim
to be in the know.

I continue devouring any material that I get my
hands on. Gerry is instrumental in this process,
providing me with material she has read and
thinks worthy of consideration. I read of alien
races, angels, psychic channeling and the likes.
It's all wildly fascinating. During this time Gerry
provides Maria, my cousin Marie and myself with
forms of meditation aimed at quieting your mind.

"It's the thoughtless state where communication
becomes possible," she would often tell me. I

practice nightly while continuing to give myself a crash course in various schools of spiritual thought. After taking a job on a roofing crew of a friend I met through music, the next significant turn occurred.

He was into eastern thought, which up until that time I knew very little about. He talked about this guy named Paramahansa Yogananda; I had never heard of him and didn't think too much of it. One day while on a job he gave me the book, "The Teachings of the Buddha," I had read a small accounting of the Buddha in Elizabeth Clare Prophet's books and was really interested to get a better more first-hand account of the Buddha. What occurred during the reading of that book was beautiful. I felt such love for the Buddha. It was as if I knew him somehow, in mind only, the middle way, detachment; it was awesome stuff, real practical in its application. Of course there were the ridiculous assertions common to any organized religion, but I had unknowingly begun a process of recognizing what rang true to me and what was bogus in my eyes. The Buddha I felt this love for was my unique perspective through said process of discernment.

The beat goes on. While reading a book one day, on the shitter, having to do with angels and guides

I came across a reference from Carlos Santana. He was talking about Jesus, Buddha and Krishna being great lights. "Who's this Krishna guy?" I thought. If he was anything at all like Jesus and Buddha I had to find out all I could about him. I went to the bookstore a couple of days later on a mission. While approaching the doors something that I can only describe as completely bizarre took place. The entirety of my field of vision changes and I was looking into the face of an Indian man. He spoke, "You will buy my book today." Looking back I should have realized I was in trouble, up until that point everything was hunky dory. I would meditate, get some messages, or at least imagine I was and continue on with my life unabated.This was something entirely new. But blind with an obsessive, insatiable thirst to become spiritually realized, I was empowered by the experience. I entered the bookstore still not really knowing much about Krishna but figuring if there was anything to be found, it would be found in the new age theology section. I look; I see books written by someone named Krishnamurti but no plain Krishna. I'm not really sure of anything, that might be the guy but I keep on looking. I happen to see a book by Paramahansa Yogananda, That's the guy Jeff talked about. I pick it up and nearly shit my pants; it's the Indian cat I just saw when I was walking into the bookstore. Too freaky to ignore I decide Krishna can wait and purchase "Autobiography of a Yogi. "What the fuck is a yogi?" I wonder, guess I'm going to find out. I pour through the pages reading one after another, the supernatural accounts of the great spiritual prowess of these yogis. This is totally and utterly intoxicating to me, these guys are the real deal it seems. I'm completely obsessed with becoming a master of God realization that they purport to be. Upon completion I send for the home lessons referred to in the back of the book and feel the tremendous excitement of anticipation. "This is what I've been searching for!"

It was during this time that I began what I can only think to term, through a referential mindset of sports, an intense training regimen. I quit drinking, quit smoking pot and even quit cigarettes cold turkey without as much as a thought of it. I was on a mission. Every two weeks two more lessons would arrive and I was always eager to see what new discipline they would bring in hopes that it would ultimately engender the awareness I was completely obsessed with becoming. They spoke of the mind faculties be likened unto a radio, where diligent practices of their method would bring about a fine tuning of said faculties to that of God. For all intent and purposes I became a monk within my own self, created ashramic bubble that was 118 Harrisburg Street. I even gave up thought of ever engaging in any sort of sexual intimacy again. As I look back now there was one problematic issue I was faced with but chose to overlook. Their claim of being not only the fastest but the one and only means of achieving God realization. Remember what I said about being wary of those who claim to be in the know, most especially those who claim sole ownership of truth. I don't mean to sound too hard on Self Realization Fellowship, Church Triumphant and Elizabeth Clare Prophet make the same assertions as well as countless others. Anyway I continued with their techniques and began to notice some measure of success, or so I thought.

For the next couple of years I adhered to my strict regimen, often times meditating as much as three times a day. There were many perceptions, a good many of which proved verifiable and like the good little fishy that I was, I took the bait every time always thirsting for more in a state of blind obsession. I should come clean though, my intentions and goals were evolving in consonance with my awareness. I would often pray both while deep in meditation and in my waking life, "God please wake me up, I'll do whatever it takes to help

heal all." Then it begins, while in meditation one
morning now prior to work, which incidentally
was a courier job, a vision which I can only liken
unto an interactive movie played before my inner
sight in remarkable clarity. In it I am some sort of
knight; I'm dressed in armor and seated in a small
boat. Directly in front and just above me I become
aware of a presence, it speaks to me. "Are you
ready?" "Yes," I respond instinctively, with my
response the boat begins to float gently down the
stream as the song goes. I come to an area that is
an array of numerous natural pools. To my right
there is a pit, in it are a group of people many of
whom I recognize. Then suddenly my attention
is brought back to the pools, there are sharks and
crocs and all sorts of dangerous creatures in them.
They're circling about me as I wade in. Suddenly
a bright royal blue eel, like a serpent appears
in the water maneuvering through the array of
creatures. Without thought I launch the spear
I'm brandishing into the water at the eel, it's a
hit. I pull it up out of the water and suddenly feel
this is not something to be feared, it's something
I need and with the dawning of that recognition
I pull it off the spear hold it up in my right hand
and turn to the pit and declare to those in it,
"I've got it!" Next the scene shifts and I am seated
in the boat once more near a shoreline where a
silhouette of what appears to be the Buddha is

seated in meditation. With that the vision is gone as abruptly as it came.

I proceed with the training as I have termed it until the required time elapses where I am now eligible for the final phase of the home schooling course, the supposed Holy Grail, Kriya Yoga. I contact SRF and petition for receiving the teaching I've sought. What happens next is downright freaky by anyone's standards. Gerry calls me from her loft in Maple Court and informs me that a message has been left on her machine from somebody at SRF. Not to freaky yet? Well wait and see. I go to Gerry's and listen to the message. It is a monotone voice that says "Michael . . . Andrew Michael Lawless . . ." it goes on to identify itself as Bramacharya Kirk, and relays that I should contact him in regards to their dissemination of Kriya. Here's the freaky part, they never had Gerry's telephone number. I never so much as even communicated to them her existence. I know what you're thinking, caller I.D. Wrong I never called there from her number, how did they have it or know that I could be reached there? Her number is unlisted and private and does not appear on any caller I.D. Gerry and I are freaked a little to say the least. I return home and contact Kirk or Captain Kirk as I would humorously dub him later in my

state of lunacy. He informs me there were some
inconsistences with my perspective versus theirs
on my Kriya application and that I would need
more practice before I could receive their consent
and subsequent dissemination of the method.
I was totally bummed. Typical now I came to
think, it's all about control with religious groups.
I reluctantly accept his assessment and move
forward. But what you're going to become privy
to is the fact that I'm a stubborn lil' ole mule and
there's always more than one way to skin a cat.

I'm over at Gerry's and she has just purchased
a book from an author named Norman Paulsen
entitled "Christ Consciousness." The author was
a student under direct tutelage of Paramahansa
Yogananda and not only recounts the amazing
adventure that is his path to realization but states
his Solar Lagos Foundation will provide any
who seek , with the technique of meditation that
parallels Kriya Yoga. Paydirt! After completing
the book Gerry and I send for their instructional
tape and corresponding booklet. Norman's a
real bro, I felt an instant kinship with him while
reading and contemplating his accounts and look
at that people, no control, he gives it freely to
anyone who seeks.

*I begin practicing his technique but as much as
I felt love for the guy, I begin to see it wasn't
necessary for my realization. I was already
unfolding at an alarming rate or was I? What
happens next is in and of itself thoroughly
evidential of the insanity that was now more
and more laying claim to my awareness. I'm in
meditation practicing the hong sau technique
taught by SRF, after it was all said and done
this was my favorite, while focusing the recess of
my mind in prayer and continuing the up-front
conscious mantra. I pray deeply to God to
realize me so that I may be as Jesus or Buddha
and liberate those imprisoned when suddenly
what would seem to be a horrific vision to most,
occupies my inner sight. I see myself on the cross.
I'm not fazed by it though as I remain in a state
of placid detachment. Then not so much as a voice
but the communication of a complete thought
comes to me as clear and plain as the nose on
my face, "There is a price to be paid." Without
hesitation I immediately respond to the thought,
"I accept," I declare. What am I fucking nuts?
Of course, and I offer you this as absolute proof,
who in their right mind would agree to such
a thing? I'm not in what can be termed "right
mind" though apparent enough. I recall reading
Neale Donald Walsch's Conversations with God
books, most specifically an excerpt that discusses*

the matter of free will. In short the supposed God delivering those communications asserts his will is our will however our will is not necessarily his will and continues that nobody does his will all of the time. Well that sounded like a challenge being laid down to me so I throw down the gauntlet and indignantly professed, "I'll be that hump, I'll do God's will all the time." And so as I adapted SRF's affirmation of "I will will, act and reason but guide thou my will action and reason to the right thing I should do, "to that which struck me as the ultimate affirmation Jesus ever laid down. "Not my will Father, but thine will be done." As I said I'm a stubborn lil' ole mule most especially when someone tells me there's something I can't do! And so the stage was set for what I would come to refer to as the darkest night of the soul I would ever experience. I had even laid on the back burner all thoughts of my musical career in a stance of complete and total surrender or so I thought. What ensued was the beginning of insanity or perhaps the continuance and intensification thereof.

6
The Battle Begins

Money is tight at home, my mother refinances the house to satisfy a considerable debt to the I.R.S., bloodsuckers, but she does it with a flexible interest rate. Consequently, the payments escalate and we're really getting in over our heads. It's a race against time to prepare the house for sale while trying to hold on. I do the best I can to help her hold it together but the process off my undoing is well under way. I fix what needs to be done to the house, continue to work my part time courier gig and pick up work with Jeff roofing and siding in the afternoons until evening. All the while I continue my meditation and energization regimen morning and night. I continue to pray but upon conclusion of all prayer and often throughout the days I affirm, "not my will Father but thy will be done." Thought word deed right Neale. I'm burning the candle at both ends already dangling on the precipice of lunacy. It was during this time that I enlisted myself in a most dangerous endeavor of practice. I realized that for some time now or so I thought I could hear other's thoughts. Stupidly enough I began to address consciously and audibly the issues and concerns. I was

receiving these thoughts I would later term the
collective unconscious.

*I'm asleep but aware, I'm dreaming of a head
appearing to me, it looks like me with short hair.
Currently I look like a common representation of
Jesus and am teased thusly, I recognize it from
a frame of reference books I've digested along
the way, its St. Germain. There's an expression
of deep sadness on his face, then I wake. In the
delirium that's come to be my system of logical
reasoning I surmise that I am he, the master
I've always sought to be It makes perfect sense
to my reasoning mind, which is now hanging on
by a thread if anything. Of course I surmise, he's
a representative of the Holy Spirit, the thought
adjuster referred to in "The Urantia Book," it's
my role to receive and subsequently balance these
thoughts that are coming to me, it's my destined
role. And with that conclusion the thread that
precariously held me however frailly to reality
is severed. I'm completely at the mercy of that
which I now identify as the collective unconscious,
a place where no vestige of truth exists. I cut
my hair and proceed forward in the seeming
knowingness that I am he.*

*I lay in my bed: sleep is now becoming more
rare and farther in between. A peace overcomes*

me however momentarily; I associate this with the presence of God. "I'll give all that I am to all Father," I profess and with this admission my field of vision slowly transforms to a total white out. It's already too late for me now there is no basis in reality left I identify this as my ascension. And thusly my sight returns and I drift off to sleep. It is now 1999 yet I am still 28 years old, my birthday is later that year and all that I held sacred as my identity is about to come crashing down around me.

Moment by moment I'm becoming more radical and assertive in my new found awareness. I turn my thoughts to the horrors of the world, China in Tibet, the most recent Gulf War; I focus myself proclaimed thought adjusting to highlight the similarities in all theology I have studies along the way. The Koran, Torah, The Dhammapada, The New Testament, the Bhagavad Gita, it's my own little delusional messianic mission to unite the faiths of the world. By this time I'm speaking aloud in retort to the cacophony that has claimed my mind. I wrestle with it fervently but I'm losing and am headed further into the abyss. Gerry is concerned for me. She cautions me not to dabble in this practice I've dubbed my destiny, I pay no heed, I'm now dwelling in the ego's realm all the while thinking I'm fulfilling some sort of divine *purpose, I'm a goner! It's at this time I make a most erroneous assessment that will ultimately lead to anguish, pain and torment the likes of which I've never experienced. I'm about to go over the edge entirely, through one big final choice assumption. In the psychotic realm that has become my mind I think I have found Portia, Germain's, my twin flame. Does such a concept already exist, yes but I've always known it to be Gerry, but now I don't even exist in the ozone layer of reality much less the same universe and I've severed ties with the only person who could possibly be of any help bringing me back from it.*

It's at this time that what I come to identify as the dimensional jumps or jaunts start taking place. It's subtle at first; I feel a strange sensation of differentiation preceded by an eerie silence each time. Things on the surface appear to be the same but there's a looming awareness that something is substantially different. I now become aware of a personality presence or energy awareness; through the frame of reference that was my self-administered education. I identify it as Sanat Kumara. In the series of distorted thought patterns that is now the psychosis of my mind, I realize his was the embodiment of Socrates. I channel what I perceive to be this awareness and come to the realization that sooner or later we all are subject to fulfilling the will of God and consequently his plan. It is most strongly characterized in the affirmation which has come to be my home stay with a completely irreverent twist namely, "Not my will Father but thine be done; after all you're the fucker who made me." "Well pardon me for fucking cursing but you're the fucker who made me Father, thy will be done. If it be not thy fucking will Father, then sure as all fucking shit it couldn't be done. After all you're the crazy fucker who made me; well fuckin' forgive fucking me Father, thy fuckin' will be done." I'm now madder than all hell and I don't mean angry, I'm totally gone, yet it's the most beautifully, liberating experience I've ever felt. This awareness is totally content within itself contemplating the nature of being in a total state of delirium with not even the slightest hint of a fear of consequence. And with this starts the experiences of death. I see death for what it is, a simple transformation, reorientation and correspondingly a rejuvenation of the awareness referred to in Hinduism as atman, in Buddhism as mind or in western thought that which is identified as soul. I'm ranting and raving, quite happily I must say, all the while jaunting from dimension to dimension, I collapse and recollect my faculties dying again and again all the while in what I dub the little box. I'm laughing *hysterically through most of it while the Alice in Chains song, "Man in the Box," plays in my mind. I surmise to myself that God has put me in some sort of trans-dimensional bubble or "box" that is the empty apartment upstairs in my house and is for some reason holding me up as some sort of crazy example for all the evolutionary spheres. I've gone beyond the point of turning back, thoroughly embracing the insanity I've become with not as much as even a thought of ever returning. With this complete relinquishment of all we view as reality an insight comes to the fore, Portia's in trouble, she'll die without me. I know, I know, I'm not in much of a position to help anyone much less myself, but in the insanity that has now become the true reality for me. I must act quickly and decisively. I start to pursue her but in complete and utter desperation, I've got to get to her before she dies, and not as I have been, but for good. It is up to us to put an end to all the needless bloodshed. The poor girl who's become the object of my focus understandably gets freaked out by the relentless pursuits that are my misguided sense of urgency and recoils in fear. In all that has ever transpired in these experiences, this is the one that will stand up as the greatest transgression I am guilty of. I never so much as went out of my way to pursue any woman, it always happened quite naturally for me, and as aforementioned this still stands to date as that which I am least equipped to forgive myself of. Not only have I scared the shit out of her, but I have subjected Gerry, the one whom I truly love to a death all her own as she helplessly stands by bearing witness to the insanity I have now become embodiment of. I'm now well out there beyond the lunatic fringe. The date is now 27, April 1999 and I'm about to suffer some serious consequences of my misguided delusional mind.*

I wrap up rehearsal at my bass players house, obvious to him never really being there and go off in search of this imagined Portia. I go to the house of a friend's brother where I met her and know she's staying, knock on the front door; my friend's brother comes to the door. I ask for her, he tells me she doesn't want to see me, go home. I turn around and get back in my car, he doesn't understand the urgency here, she will die without me! With that thought I hear a woman's voice in my head say, "if he doesn't go to the back door he'll be waiting all of his life." My sense of urgency now intensifies and I get out of my car go through the side gate around to the back and knock at the back door. My friend's brother is freaked out now too, faced with that reaction a pang hits me and even in the total state of insanity which is now "the real" for me, I know this is wrong and leave. I get home go inside for a second and then go out in the driveway. No sooner am I standing out there the four SCPD cruisers pull up. They ask me to identify myself; I do and am immediately cuffed. "What's the charge?" I ask. "Trespassing," he proclaims and proceeds to stuff me in the back of the cruiser and off to the third precinct we go. I'm rattled in disbelief for a moment. "No." I declare to myself, "I'm the ascended master Saint Germaine, I will remain poised, there's a greater hand at work here. "not my will Father, but thine be done." And so I find a calm refuge in the insanity that is my mind. I'm brought to the precinct and sat down for questioning, I'm in no mood for any sort of authority questioning my motives, I'm the ascended master Saint Germain after all, God is the authority I answer to and I am of course an extension thereof. I'm difficult to say the least, not giving him the answers he wants but rather fucking with him, jarring him off balance with riddle like word play in the utter immersion of that which has become my reality. The Lieutenant comes out, "Andrew, I worked under your father; we're trying to help you." The plea falls on deaf ears, I'm too far gone within the self-deluded maze that is my identification as the authority here. "What is this good cop bad cop?" I say, "No, we're trying to help you!" he reiterates. In my mind in the flash that is a momentary instant, I recall the words of Mohandas Gandhi, "What I do is not out of want of respect for authority, but rather is in adherence to a higher truth." I laugh at him; there's a greater hand at work here. "Not my will Father but thine be done." I'm in no mood for compliance. With that they take me into an observation room and cuff me to the desk. I know they're watching me from the next room but I don't care. I look down at the side of the desk where I spot the date 12/13 carved into it. My father's birthday, it's a sign I surmise and dad is with me. "I'm not alone I declare." The collective unconscious of their minds assails me. "I hear you!" I exclaim. Now they're really convinced I'm nuts and with one last phone call and the consent of a friend of the family, also a police officer, we're off to see the wizard. "Where are we going?" I ask. "It should be a walk in the park," the patrolman who brought me in says. I'm put back in the patrol car and off to Stony Brook University Hospital we go. Along the way I'm awestruck by the beautiful sepia like sky. I will not stray from the Father's will, which for me is the main body of contemplation; I'm the hump that does every time. I'm brought in and the girl who's the attendant on duty takes the necessary information from me, she's wearing her hair pulled back in a purple scrunchy. "I like your scrunchy," I tell her. Saint Germain, the

violet flame. I offer her no resistance complying
with each request for background information.
Next I'm brought into a little room where several
doctors sit in front and around me. "What's your
name?" asks the female doctor who appears to me
to be from India. "I am the one and the many,"
I respond. Rest assured even at this time in this
state of mind, I'm well aware of my name and
the expected answers to the subsequent questions,
but I am surrounded by the permeating feeling
that was that of Jesus whilst being brought before
the Pharisees and Sadducees. Beside I am here
to help liberate them not the other way around,
at least that's the mindset. And to add to the
madness, she's Indian, she should understand
where I'm coming from. "What's the date and
time?" she continues. I'm well aware it's April 28,
1999, 3:30am, but I'm not willing to back down
just yet. "I don't subscribe to time," I tell her,
"it's a man-made construct, not an absolute, and
is subject to various interpretation therin." I'm
going to tell you three things to remember and
I'm going to ask you to repeat them back to me
in a few minutes," she says, "a wall, the door and
a pencil." She continues with her observational
inquires all the while I offer not as much as one
answer she's looking for. She finally asks me to
recount the three things she told me to remember.
"A wall, the door and I forgot the third one," I

state. "It's a pencil, "she says. "Exactly," I respond, "I am a pencil in God's hands," I offer quoting Mother Theresa. They had all they needed, an orderly or nurse approaches me and hits me with an injection of what I probably now figure to be Ativan. "Forgive them Father for they know not what they do," is my response. "Oh God, I feel like I'm in church," exclaims one orderly in a tone of sarcastic condescension. "All of creation is a church, brother," is my immediate response. And with that I'm brought into a holding room where everyone exits but those attending, the door locks and I am faced with a harsh dose of reality, these fuckers aren't letting me go! I pace back and forth while rage builds up inside of me. Slowly the tranquilizer takes hold as I struggle against it, trying to remain conscious. "Resist not evil," is the thought that comes to me and in acquiescence to the master's teaching from whence the thought came I lie down and go completely unconscious.

The following morning I'm transported by ambulance to St. John's Hospital in Smithtown. My awareness has regained its footing and whilst delusion regains control I consider the name of the hospital and the symbolism is not lost on me. The revelator! In a reeling attempt to maintain some sense of a grip over the situation, my demented mind theorizes that this is the karmic

load I must bear, I must prevent the revelations
from occurring. It's quite apparent that my ego
knows no bounds; of what import is some two
bit guitarist from a tiny hamlet on Long Island,
so self-deluded to claim dominion over such a
supposed event through preventive action. I go
along with their treatment for the first day until
I acquaint myself with the patient's bill of rights.
Rule number 6 will be the ground on which I make
my stand often times in the years to come.

6. Patient has the right to refuse treatment,
examination and/or observation.

Pretty cut and dry to me, it's my interpretation
that gives me the right to walk A.M.A. Such is
not the case according to them. I make various
calls of inquiry seeking legal representation but
am ultimately faced with the fact that I must
use the provided public defender. I meet with
her on the appointed day and provide her with
some literature that will provide some sort of
insightful background into the indignantly
defiant insanity that I am. The court date
comes for treatment over objection and I am
transported to the facilities of the New York
State Supreme Court, pertaining to the legislation
of mental hygiene. My hands were somewhat
tied in this matter, the court documents were

fraudulent stating I broke down the back door
to the house that night, a claim made falsely by
my friend's brother and when I broached the
subject of with my attorney furnishing reference
in the New York State Penal Code that was
my father's (I had my mother bring me dad's
edition) she informed me it was not relevant
in a court of mental hygiene. "The hell it's not!"
was my thought. There it was right in front of
me in black and white, fraud in the first degree,
fraudulent assertions in a court document, to
no avail. I should have won before the shit ever
started. I wasn't licked yet though. The trial
begins, doctors give their testimony as to how I
require medication, citing loads of bullshit, then
comes my turn. "Not my will Father; but thine be
done." I take the stand and my attorney serves
up questions I answer one by one calmly and
then comes the kicker. You must understand, I'm
still coming from the delusive viewpoint of the
ego, feeling it's my mission to prove something
and it is within the framework of that mindset
that I consider my response to the final query
put to me. "Do you intend to make contact with
this young woman again if you are released?" it
was mine to win all I had to do was say what I
really intended but that wasn't good enough for
me. I was making my stand on some delusional
teaching with its supposed origin as God. In a

momentary flash I gather my response. I've
been served no papers to date stating there are
any legalities preventing me from seeing her
and I think of the self-proclaimed messenger
of God's word, Neale Donald Walsch and my
response is similarly defiantly based in the
perspective of delusion. "No I respond, unless
I change my mind." My attorney's head falls
into her hands and in the end case scenario I'm
remanded to custody of the hospital where I'm
to be administered treatment over objection in
the form of injection if I refuse to voluntarily
follow the treatment plan. Still full of piss and
vinegar in the form of indignation, I refuse
treatment and am hit with several injections a
day for the next couple of days. They administer
no counteracting agent and within these few
short days, I have a massive reaction to the
injections. My whole body cramps and an
uncontrollable seizure over comes me. The nurses
scramble to administer the counteracting drug
Cogentin and while it was a scary scenario the
symptoms abate. I finally go along with their
plan. Within two days an officer arrives at the
hospital to present me with a restraining order of
protection issued at this young woman's request.
It's legal now and I will never as much as think
of looking her way again, much less violating
it. I would use this as justification later in my

distortions I considered reasoning. They had me on trespassing was the thought, fair enough but being Saint Germaine whose twin flame is the goddess of justice, it was my destined mission to take on the so called scales of justice in a visible rendering of the corruption therein. Due process, in my perspective had failed. My ego is quite adept at the manipulations of data as a means of achieving its own ends. But quite truthfully, once you're in the system, it's the automatic assumption your incapable of knowing what's best for you and consequently, have very little footing if at all any rights, which would become torturously obvious in the later accounts. I continue with the prescribed treatment and am released two and a half weeks later.

I'm all fucked up over it, nobody treats me the same and their judgment is raining down on me from all sides. I can see it in their faces, all but one, my beloved Gerry. In the aftermath of such a traumatic experience I'm brought back down to Earth. "I'm no master," I would often think to myself, "I'm a psycho and my life has been completely devastated." I was torn apart badly, wounded in a way worse than ever before. All that I had built my life on was destroyed in one foul swoop. Still I wasn't ready to buy into the doctor's diagnosis of bipolar disorder. I threw out the medications, Depakote, Haldol, Cogentin all flushed down the toilet. I would find some measure of relief in my music. I began focusing on writing original compositions. "I'm no messiah," I would often think but, "I can still play a mean guitar and carry a tune," my music once again would ultimately save me.

7
Round Two, the Ego Reasserts Itself

I start to spend some of my time recounting what and where I went wrong. I consider the teachings I absorbed in the training I underwent. Thought word deed comes to the fore in my mind, another great big heaping pile of horse shit is revealed for what it is. Tell that to the bum in the gutter trying to beg a few dollars for a fix what it is. "Don't sweat it brother, as I ain't got money for you I got something better, the truth from none other than God himself. You got yourself into it now all you've got to do is think yourself out of it. You can do it, come on now; thought word deed, come on now I'm pulling for you, you have the same dynamo of creative power as God, I know he told me. "What a crock of shit, with this thought comes the birth of another. It occurs to me that God's so called messenger is now filthy stinking rich from purveying his song and dance. And what's so new about it. I mean the Buddha summed the whole thing up in one statement when he declared, "we are the result of all of our thoughts and actions." I'm the psycho here but this guy's publicly claiming to have had a conversation with

God that was totally initially to be a trilogy, but it must not have been enough money or notoriety. I guess God must have changed his mind but all that line got me was shot full of dope. Sorry to bash you Neale but a fellow egomaniac is an easy make at this point in time.

And as the saying goes, you become that which you judge. Gerry's tenderness provides the gentle inclination toward healing. I spent most of my time at the loft with her and slowly but surely have given up the only thing I needed to give up all along, concern for the judgment of others. We grow even closer than before as she tends to my wounded psyche. Little by little I begin to emerge again. I'm constantly confronted and assailed with and by a paralyzing fear from within. I put all my trust in God and got rocked, or did I. It seems my ego is a more worthy adversary than even I could have imagined. Neale Donald Walsch has got nothing on me. Little by little the ego reasserts itself through the means of justification. It was a karmic blow I took for the good of all, I tell myself, I am the master Saint Germain. Slowly but surely, in small increments the insanity begins the process of reclamation. I overcome the fear that has plagued me to some extent and begin the assertion of my beloved affirmation, "Not my will Father but thine be done." The transformation is

39

accelerated this time as lunacy bullies itself to the
fore of my mind.

I'm driving in my car headed for Captree
overlook; it's a sacred location to me. Its night
I'm not sure what time and I don't much care.
As I approach the bridge I see it's still under
construction. Upon arrival at the bridge
something weird happens that would recur over
the years. My field of vision goes completely black,
I'm not sure at this point in time if the bridge
is even intact. I feel a pang of fear that is shock
within this void. I ignore it and a total sense of
calming peace comes over me with this peace I
emerge from the blackness and am acutely aware
that once again I've just skipped dimensions.
My mind is confounded by the experience, have
I crossed over I wonder, did I die? Maybe the
bridge was out and I've crossed over without
even knowing it. In all honesty I don't know
what the truth is other than the fact that I just
went through some portal into a different Long
Island. I reach the overlook parking lot, park the
car and head for the shore. As I get there I start
running, I'm not even sure why other than the
fact that I'm running toward not away from
something. In my mind's eye I see the projection
of two masters behind me, I intuitively know who
they are without really knowing why. It's the

ascended masters, Morya and Victory; they flank
me to the rear on either side. I'm getting fatigued
and I fall to the sand in exhaustion. They help me
up and I begin running again, I'm keenly aware
of a knowingness that this run is symbolic of my
mission and it will take all I have to complete. I
reach my destination, an outcropping and feel
the presence of God. My two brothers remain just
behind and to either side of me, they're standing
with me. I'm not alone in this. Without any
thought I instinctively say to the presence I feel is
God," I'm ready." I begin my return to the car and
as I draw nearer to the bridge I enter the water
and baptize myself three times in succession,
once for John the Baptist, once for Jesus and
once for James the Just, the brother of Christ. I
take the violet Buddha hat Gerry bought me and
cast it into the water. This will be a mission of
my own unique styling not that of Buddha. Once
again I identify myself as the awareness that is
Saint Germain. I return home and descend to my
basement temple.

The collective unconscious rages through my mind
in stereo, you would think I'd be a little wise to its
game but it's like a drug I can't get enough of. I'm,
addicted to this alternate reality. I start ranting
at the collective unconscious again, this time my
mother and sister drop a dime on me, they call the

mobile crisis unit and I'm paid a visit. The woman enters the house and asks me to sit and talk with her. I do so reluctantly and she looks me square in the eyes. What happens next freaks me out, there's no denying it I'm out on a limb again, but this time I see her as some sort of alien being in human form, a phenomena that would be revisited many times. She stares into my eyes assaulting me with the most paralyzing fear I've ever felt, I'm of the mind that she's doing it on purpose and I can't hold her gaze. "No," I shout and get up and walk outside, she follows shorty after and as she exits my house my mind perceives the thought that she is every bit as entitled to be that which she is as I. I fall to my knees and prostrate myself before her as she comes down the ramp. She smiles and goes to her car, gets in and drives off with her partner. I return to the basement temple and within a minute am confronted by two police officers. They order me to get up, I ignore them, then the one doing the talking says, "civil disobedience is good," and with that they each grab me under the arms and drag me out. I'm cuffed once again, stuffed in the cruiser and as you can well imagine I'm off to see the wizard once again. What happens next is sheer horror for me. After being admitted and vitals checked they drag me into a secluded room, strap me to a bed in four point restraints and hit me with a massive injection. I'm now screaming in terror, "no please not the cross, please, not the cross." They now exit the room and I'm left to my own devices as the sedative takes root. "These alien fuckers are studying me, I didn't do anything wrong, I've hurt no one, why the cross." my breathing slows down and becomes more labored as I lay my head back and look into the light. "This isn't happening again," I say "why me Father, Why?"

I awake in a drug induced slumber, I stumble to the door in front of me, through the glass I see my little sister, she's pacing back and forth and can't escape, "leave her alone," is the cry that emerges from within me, these fuckers are coming after us, this time the placidity of patience is nowhere to be found. I'm pissed off beyond all recognition. Consciousness abates and I'm out again. I wake in a bed in Southside Hospital 2 north and am startled at who I see. It's a nurse who is the spitting image of Jane Roberts, the author of the Seth books, for some silly ass reason I'm speaking in an Irish brogue and I'm calling her Jane. The rage has given way to peace thanks to Jane and I'm now faced with the prospect of another legal battle. It's late December and this will be the first of two Christmas' and New Years I spend in a psych ward, It's the new millennium and here I sit. It would end up being a most interesting stay, though. The shit of it all is I didn't so much mind the incarcerational aspect of these stays so long as my mind was left to be. It's like that saying that's attributed to the angelic presence that is Nisroc, "stone walls a prison do not make if you be free in your mind." But ultimately that wouldn't be the case. During this visit I take up smoking again. I come up with all sorts of sayings, like." Smoke the fire became the fire, that's a grok." Many of the people both staff and patients are symbolic to me of the masters I've read about in the preceding years. I make an associative account of Norman Paulsen, an orderly who I now come to associate as Serapis Bey, Prince Moishe is one of my fellow patients who through the scope of the insanity that I 'm in, is also an embodiment of Sanat Kumara, another fellow patient is to me in my form of symbolic association John the Baptist or as I have affectionately dubbed him "El Baptismo" and lastly The Dalai Llama is represented by a patient I refer to as Clifford the big red dog. Believe you me, I'm well aware of how crazy this sounds but I assure you I'm completely harmless within this insanity that is my mind.

I'm on what they call a one to one. They're treating me as if I'm the same sort of violent criminal, when in all this time the only thing I can be said to be guilty of was trespassing. Was

there not indeed a reference made to such by
the great master we have all come to regard so
highly? While on this one to one I recall within my
mind, "One flew over the cuckoo's nest." I pick up
a chair and contemplate throwing it through the
window. A male nurse who I must admit has been
quite kind to me since admission comes running
in at the request of the one to one orderly and
pleads with me to put the chair down. I consider
the ultimate hilarity of the situation for truly I'm
now completely immersed in the belief, that I am
Saint Germain and as Yogananda would put it,
am simply acting out a part in the cosmic movie.
I never intended to throw it, I'm simply fucking
around in some state of delirium. Of course I'm
not going to throw it, I'm on the second floor and
there's no escape. I laugh and put it down, this
charade lands me in restraints, confirming and
warranting their approach with a complementary
injection and I'm out. When I wake I'm out of
restrains, Southside was actually one of the more
hesitant facilities with regard to this barbaric
practice. It is at this point a phenomenon
referenced earlier resurfaces. The kind male
nurse asks me if I want to play chess with him.
He walks with a limp and appears almost to
have a knee that is in the wrong direction. The
memory of the movie The Arrival comes to
mind only that's not quite right. This is a most

benevolent being before me. I agree to play and move with him to the dining area and sit down to play. We employ vastly different techniques mine defend the queen at all cost, his utilize her superior prowess. I have a warm easy feeling and my mind eases while a realization dawns in me. This is my brother from long ago and he's come to help me. Needless to say he wins and as he gets up to leave the room he says, "You've got to utilize the queen," looking into my eyes. I become aware of the message he's giving me, Gerry should be utilized. But in the delusionary mind that I am, I will not let her enter this fight, I'll take it on and win keeping her out of it. I spend most of my time there walking up and down the halls, all the while exercising number six on the patient's Bill of Rights, until one night when I'm denied that simple luxury. The head nurse stands at the door of my room and orders me to stay in there. "I'm not doing anything wrong I just want to walk," is my response, as I try to walk around him. He pushes me back in the room, I regroup and walk forward again, this time he grabs me twisting my arm to the point of a near break, at the last second I adjust the position of my body relative to his assault as to avoid serious injury. He throws me in the isolation room, no idea why this is happening but in the insanity that is my mind, I view it as some form of training. While in

there I go on a mind trip ultimately annihilating
the concept of space. It all looks the same there
and I realize space's illusory properties. With
that I go on some freaky mind trip that they're
administering lethal gas to me, flooding the room
with it. But in this trip I begin to realize the
advantages of being the self-proclaimed Saint
Germain, I'm immortal already, even if I haven't
died yet which is the more entertained possibility.
I decide I'll maintain the appearance of around 26
years old, Saint Germaine doesn't age. They finally
let me out and I return to my room.

Within the next couple of days, they move me
into a room with Clifford the big red dog, the jolly
Dalai Llama. It's good at first but he's a crazy
little Dalai Llama with a bad temper. One night
while both of us are in our room I'm most deadly
in the Gaseous Clay department, that is to say I'm
farting and they reek. Clifford has had enough
and gets quite animated in insisting I not do it
again. I laugh and can't help it and let one go,
Clifford has had enough and snaps. He picks up
the heavy wooden chair and is threatening me
with it. There's no reaction from me at all, rather
I go within my mind and petition Sanat Kumara,
or Prince as I've come to affectionately refer to
him, to protect me. I don't move a muscle, I make
no effort to protect myself, still seated on the bed

47

with hands by my side, I put my total trust in Prince to protect me. Then Clifford winds up and swings, it's a direct hit crashing against my head just over my right eye. I'm knocked backwards but not out, I see red and in a fit of rage. get up to my feet and start towards him, he recoils in sheer terror of disbelief that I've gotten up. He jumps back on the bed and in an instant the total fear he displays subdues my anger. I can't hurt him, it's not me. I back up and with that the staff comes rushing in and Clifford is moved to a different room and placed in four point restraints for a good while. The blow opened up my eyebrow and requires seven stitches to close. I don't let them administer a local or any sort of anesthetizing agent other than cleansing. Pain I tell myself is just another sensation, assign nothing to it, it is neither good nor bad. In the aftermath of that incident through my faculties of insane reasoning I surmise it was another karmic blow I've taken on. The realization is that Clifford, being the Dalai Llama, is still a little boy. He was placed in a monastery at a young age and is quite frustrated at the weighty responsibilities thrust upon him. In some way I've eased the Dalai Llama's suffering.

The next association I would make would apparently provide me with more experimental evidence to further justify my insanity. A new patient comes in and is on a one to one. He's a cute little guy that gives me a warm feeling. As I walk up and down the hall I take notice of his almost robotic discipline as he lays perfectly still in his bed while being supervised. He's apparently perfectly content without any sort of reaction to being confined to his room, he barely moves, his name is William. Later while in group the association forms in my mind bringing me said justified madness in the form of a past life. I'm looking upon William with a warm sense of amusement when it comes on; the experience is that of an awareness all around me, then I see it. It's the picture of Yogananda as a younger boy, the recognition becomes immediate. "Oh my God," I think, "I was Sri Yuketswar in my last incarnation." It's perfectly logical to the unreasoning mind I've always been drawn to him of all their gurus. Some days later, delusion picking up speed now, we're in group again and Nurse Jane Roberts as I think of her asks, "Does anyone know why they're in here?" "I do," I say, "I Think I'm here to tell that little guy I love him," I say pointing to William feeling a sense of peace in the distorted mind that is "truth" to me, I've just satisfied some sort of karmic debt.

It's now that the worm starts to turn, in as much as I can't stand being caged anymore. My buddy

comes to visit me on his way upstate to go skiing.
I was supposed to go with him. Everybody's
gearing up their millennium plans and I'm stuck
in here. Even though Saint Germaine's a crazy
little Saint Germain, he is after all the master
of freedom and wants to have some fun. Prince
who was released flew off the handle and is now
back in the joint with me, John and Clifford.
He snapped because of what happened to me I
reason, it wasn't that he didn't want to protect
me it's just that he wasn't there to do it so he
freaks and starts breaking shit in his house
and gets himself thrown back in to spend the
millennium in the joint talking philosophy with
me. It's here where Price introduces me, via his
past Socratic mind, to the next level of the mind
game, which later upon its contemplation and
practice, would nearly render me in a state of
catatonic psychotic paralysis. It's the ultimate
equalizer or the "Who Knows" school of thought.
It's here where the whole thing even kicks up a
notch. If you think this is good so far, I take it to
an exponential level. But that's getting ahead of
ourselves.

My court date arrives, it's a disaster. Not only
would they pursue treatment over objection,
but there was a new twist thanks to the reverse
psychology of fear that was the powers that be.

This time they would land the big bang; Kendra's Law, mandatory outpatient medication for a period of six months. They even had the balls to cite the incident where Clifford freaked on me as proof of me being a threat to others.

8
Another Regrouping and the Seeming Victory Thereof

Apparently I'm public enemy number one for I'm assigned a most stringent supervised treatment plan that consists of a one hour visit with a shrink, a half hour therapy session and a visit to my house by a county case worker on a weekly basis. Thankfully my boss at Columbus Courier welcomes me back with open arms. The name of the company and its symbolic meaning of my distorted mind would later become further means of twisted justification in the psychosis that was my identity as Saint Germain. "Of course, I would muse from time to time. "I was Christopher Columbus, it was one on my embodiments of Germain. "As I've already stated I am the egomaniac to end all and most highly adept through the faculties of lunacy to manipulate seeming inconsequential facts for my own means. I adhere to the treatment plan reluctantly, for at this time I'm so doped us that my speech is slurred. I can hardly hold anything much less write and the greatest

*travesty of them all, cannot play guitar but am
faced with little choice, it's either that or back
to the loony bin. Slowly but surely my faculties
begin to return to me and eventually thanks
to a miracle, I work the coordination between
my mind and hands so I can play again. The
appropriate time elapses and thankfully I'm
rewarded for being a good and compliant little
nut and am now released from mandatory
status. At this juncture my body starts having an
adverse effect to the lithium that is prescribed me
in the form of vomiting often as much as several
times a day. I can't as much as brush my teeth
without throwing up. I continue with treatment
for a time however as my insanity ultimately
begins the process of a subtle regrouping within
the recess of my mind.*

*Miraculously during that time period Gerry has
managed to scrimp and save and acquires a house
in a lower income section of Bay Shore while
simultaneously the sale of my mother's house and
her subsequent move to Florida are in the works.
Gerry and I move into the house together. It's a
feeling of warm comfort and ease, though nobody
quite understands it due to our age difference, we
are very much in love with one another. Little
by little I wean myself off the medication as the
recess of my mind once again emerges and the*

alternate awareness of psychosis becomes the preferred reality. Then with an intensified and renewed vigor, comes the dimensional jaunts once again.

I'm driving in my car headed westbound on Montauk Highway from West Islip through Babylon when the blackness totally envelopes my field of vision once more. There's no fear by now however, as the phenomenon is now a regular occurrence. I emerge from the blackness with a strange comforting feeling of elation, through the new apparent advancement of the manipulation of the data in the form of signs; and their distorted meaning to me in this state of total mania. I reason, and I use that term most loosely, that I am now in the sphere of Venus, 8th density or at the octave. I continue westbound and enter West Babylon when it dawns on me I'm out of smokes and I pull into 7-11 to pick up a pack when a thought realization comes to the fore in my mind. "Strange things are a foot at the Circle K Ted." I park, get out and approach the door. As I do a woman also approaches, I hold the door open for her and smile. She looks at me directly in the eyes with a look of gentle loving understanding and seems to communicate with me telepathically, "Don't worry, you're just like us," is the thought transference. I enter the store to a scene that *cannot be adequately described in words but which I can only think to term absolute hilarity. The clerk is babbling in a total nonsensical manner and all those within are laughingly engaged and interacting with each other through the means of their own individualized forms of comedic shtick. I'm laughing with them now from a perspective of observation and approach the counter and ask for my brand of smokes. The clerk continues on with his babbling banter. I pay him and say thank you, "ba da aa bbaa bbaa la adaa your welcome," is something of his response. I exit and get back in my car and muse to myself laughing," this is the sphere of comedic freedom," I think.*

In the aftermath of this experience I feel completely free and justified in the insanity that is my mind and begin my ranting like banter adopting the Socratic mind set of complete irreverent contemplation with my own unique twist. .It is that of a foul mouthed dirty little Piggy Pen like kid, yet is one of the utter innocence. I rarely bathe if at all during this time period; oblivious to the everyday existence we call reality, existing in a universe all my own. That's simply not acceptable to those who love me, they drop the proverbial dime and by now you can guess it, I'm off to see the wizard; that is C Pep,

University Hospital of Stony Brook once more.
I'm brought in and almost instantly placed in four
point restraints but thankfully this time there is
no injection administered, that is, not yet.

While lying there in bed a dawning realization
comes on in the form of an awareness
accompanied by scenes playing in my mind's eye.
The realization is that of my lifetime as James
the Just, brother of Christ. I'm aware of the fact
Elizabeth Claire Prophet's assertions regarding
the past lives of Germain are not entirely
accurate. At least not according to my delusional
identification of the crazy little Master Germain
that is me. I remember my awareness of this fact
while reading some of her books and feeling a
pulling in my consciousness toward the seeming
fact that I was this James while reading a passage
that made brief mention of him. It seems my
insanity predates even that of my strict training.
The scenes that unfold before my inner visions
are that of a time spent in Egypt, accompanied
by John and Jeshua, which is our training in the
mystery schools in the art of the adept. I recall
the exercise of being entombed for three days and
relate it to the predicament I now find myself in,
in four points. Then it gets bad; I have to pee and
they won't let me out to relieve myself. In a flash
I see in my mind's eye the book "Zen and the Art

of Motorcycle Maintenance" "They want me to piss my pants," I think, as anger starts to build up within me. A doctor then comes in with pills and a cup of water; I refuse and am subsequently hit with an injection. It takes hold and I'm out.

I wake on a gurney as I'm being brought into Brookhaven Memorial Hospital, my next stop on the psycho mystery tour. I'm greeted by a girl I perceive to be an angel in the form of a deceased girl I knew briefly named Angela. This would be a most provocative stay. I'm currently still in alignment with the awareness I have dubbed James, it's one of absolute reverential observance of that which I would come to term the great mystery that is God. At this juncture the affirmation which is my mainstay is expanded upon in the thought form that is, "Not my will Father but thine be done. Infinitely I remain thy humble servant son, I am thy player and you are my coach. I serve thy mystery beyond reproach, all I am, I am for you, I am thy humble servant son ever true blue." Happily this is a facility that does not employ the use of restraints, only injections to assuage the turmoil of psychosis that is me and my fellow nuts. Once again the distortion that is now my very own form of reason makes many associations among those present, both staff and patients. The greatest and

foremost of which would be that of Archangel
Lucifer, a thought that strikes immediate fear in
the hearts and minds of most but I assure you that
is not the case, at least not in my own brand of
insanity, so bear with me. Another phenomenon
that has been ongoing for some years now, in the
form of apparitional flashes of light, both while
subject to medication and while not, intensifies.
I reason this is a sign from godhead concurrent
with my contemplative thoughts at said interval
of these apparitions. With each apparition I
fall to my knees and prostrate myself before
that which I have now come to think of as the
great mystery that is God. It is a practice that
draws the attention of the doctors and the staff
and will be utilized in court as a means of their
justification for treatment over objection as I once
again take refuge in number 6 in the Patient's Bill
of Rights. As night falls on a particular evening,
the night shift supervisor enters the ward and
I'm struck with the realizational awareness in
the form of my twisted associational patterned
psychosis. He looks just like Rowdy Roddy Piper,
instantly I recall in my mind the movie in which
he stared entitled "They Live." The association
engenders the delusional mindset that there
are aliens among us seeking to take over and
subjugate humanity. Rowdy salutes me as he
passes by walking to his station. I arrive at an

awareness that this is a realm of hell where those
of us here, now associated in my mind as angels,
are being subjected to all means of torment that
is the karmic debt of humanity being dispensed
by said alien race. Rowdy is non-other than the
aforementioned Lucifer who is not in the least
bit evil, but simply serving god in his destined
capacity ministering to us angels in a most kind
compassionate manner. I consider briefly the
meaning of his name; Great Light. He's showing
me, I "reason", that it is up to me to take on these
subjugating beings so as to free the angels this race
has imprisoned; with they're goal being becoming
Godhead. Simultaneously in the recess of my
mind, which is operating on many different fronts
at once, I identify myself with an awareness of
being that I perceive to be ultimate origin prior
to the incarnational rounds. It is that which
I dub Mikhaila, whose meaning to me is little
Michael, the blue ray representative of the order
Seraphim. The alien race I must confront and
ultimately defeat is identified, through my twisted
referential assignment via my self-administered
education as Ra, a self-purported ancient alien
social memory complex, highly analytical, of
supposed benevolent nature, who hails from
Venus seventh density. What ensues is battle of
epic proportions that wages within my mind
pitting the Socratic mind of the intuitive that is

me against the highly analytic mindset that is
Ra. The battle wages on for three days and nights
as I mentally dance circles around the analytical
through my now aggressive assertion that is
my own unique twist of the Socratic mind. They
tempt me to declare myself God, justifying their
power thirsting goal of achieving that very end
for themselves. I won't bite. I utilize their concept
of the One Infinite Creator to keep a footing.
Many supposed revelations come to the fore of
my totally new insanely divided mind. Memories
of Drunvalo Melchezedek become "known" as
I see I am not quite as evolved as he, rather in
Ra's purported system of soul evolution I am a
master of 12th density attainment. Another said
awareness that Ra has already begun the process
of deity via genetically engineering life to send
through the incarnational rounds for their own
twisted means of establishing themselves as
Godhead. And now they seek to lay claim to us
angels further establishing themselves as God.
During a lull in the battle, I go within in prayer
and make the ultimate assertion of the Socratic
mind in my defense of God. "Father, even if it
means the end of me for all eternity, I would die
for you," I declare in a somewhat sorrowful mind
set. On the second eve of the battle, while in the
isolation room, due to the fact that the one nurse
asked quite kindly that I go there to rant and

rave or to my room to go to sleep so as not to wake
the other patients, I am thoroughly fatigued and
collapse on the mattress. Ra, or my perception
thereof, is taunting me, claiming they will take
my body. I've nothing left in me to fight; I need a
respite so as to continue. The delusional awareness
that to me is Ra is unrelenting in its assault. I
pray, petitioning Archangel Michael to protect
me and fearfully drift off to sleep. I wake in the
morning and the battle continues from where
I left off. It's during this time frame I see the
ultimate futility of the illusion that is evolution,
choosing instead to align myself with my
perceived awareness of Mikhaila, renouncing my
evolutional status and achievements in favor of
my self-proclaimed seraphic practice of the throne.
It is now that I start the psychotic practice of
remanding them to the fire core in an attempt
to put an end to this perceived battle. They keep
coming back at me though, or such is my delusion.
Finally in a moment of peaceful clarity I feel a
presence overtake me that I identify as Archangel
Jophiel and with this awareness , my arms by
my side, bent at the elbows with palms facing
skyward my head tilts backward and I offer the
resolution to this battle in the form of an assertive
surrender and declare, "Live through me." And so
the conflict within my mind abates and I consider,

"The battle is won . . . , no the battle is One." Peace, however temporal ensues.

This however is not the end of the thoroughly conflicted insanity that is my mind for ultimately I am still at war with myself. While outside on a smoke break, another area in which this hospital is more pleasant than any other I encounter in its generosity of providing us three cigs per break, a vision comes on. In it I am on a flight deck as United States war planes and aviators are preparing for an all-out assault the likes of which has never been seen before. I become aware of a personality presence that I identify as former president George Bash. This identity looks to me in a somewhat questioning manner. I again align and identify myself to it as the insane in the membrane Germain. The questioning nature of this fragment of the unconscious persists, through the perspective of delusional insanity I surmise he is looking to me for counsel. In a flash I see the karmic ramification involved and become aware that I must delegate some of this karmic load or it will ultimately be my demise. I reluctantly nod my head granting my assent in the awareness that the United States, my very own chosen land of freedom, will be the dispenser of this karmic justice.

Upon reentering the ward a new battle arises in my most psychotic mind. I begin to consider the fact that I am the Lamb of God spoken of in the Book of Revelation, a thought that is the ultimate converse to that which up until now, has been my delusive self-proclaimed messianic mission, which was to stop the Revelation from occurring. Of course, I "reason," it says looks like a lamb. When my hair was long I looked just like Jesus, as James who was also martyred. Yes, I further substantiate, I am, Mikhaila, the first ray seraph, the first of the last, the alpha and the omega. And with this thought I go, if such a thing is possible, even further off the deep end. I am completely and utterly conflicted in this mind set and now start to rationalize that it's not up to me to take the fall in this one. The war planes in my mind now take flight as I mentally project a cloud like mist over their target area so as to further increase the ability of stealth. It's a success and the planes return as does my awareness to that of the ward. Further associations are now made through patients that are present which are; that of Stevie Ray Vaughn, a fellow foul mouthed cowboy, boot wearing southerner, that I perceive as a violet ray seraph. There's Raymond, who I "substantiate" in my lunatic mind, is Dustin Hoffman in "Rainman," a child-like man who is somewhat of a savant and is representative of Meratron to me, the mind of God. It continues. There's also a representation of my father in the form of a patient that tends to the delusional realization that my father is actually the Buddha. Again the beat goes on in the form of a patient that represents my brother, still incarnate and the subsequent assumption that he is actually John the Beloved. The ultimate insanity that is my mania knows no bounds. And then the first reference to date of my perceived days in Atlantis, through a patient that is symbolic to me of Edgar Cayce. He's an angry little Edgar however and eventually ends up assaulting me with a sucker punch, which I don't report so it can't be used against me in court this time. Lastly there's a representation of Plato that is one of the ward supervisors with whom I engage in philosophical sparring. He to me is symbolic of my deceased brother Daniel.

Finally my court date arrives and I am poised for the trial. Roddy Lucifer offers me medication that morning and I take a portion of it in good faith and as a measure of respect to him, "Tell him you want to come back," he says, "we could use a good man like you." Eventually I'm off to the Supreme Court. The trial begins, Dr. Cho, carbon-hydrogen-oxygen combustion, takes the stand and reports of my "religious preoccupation."

As he terms it and goes on to make his case of
justification.

I take the stand, conscious of my speech patterns
so as not to be accused of pressured speech and
calmly one by one answer the questions my
attorney puts to me. He breaches the topic of
"religious preoccupation," my retort is that my
belief can be summed up by the Cow 116, a passage
from the Koran. I quote it as follows, "They say
Allah hath taken unto himself a son to be glorified,
but nay, whosoever is in the heavens and earth
are his; all are subservient unto him." The judge
asks me if I will go back to work if released, which
in the time leading up to this episode is roofing
and siding for Jeff, again.

I say I will. "I don't want you wandering the
streets," he says. My testimony is completed and
miraculously the judge frees me from custody. I'm
elated, "it's over," I think, "they can't come after
me again that's double jeopardy, is the thought
however misguided. I'm transported back to the
ward where I join my brother and sister psychos
for one last round of smokes and am then released.
On the ride home I tell my mother and sister not
to come after me again but as you will come to
see, that wouldn't be the case.

9
The Goose is on the Loose

Perspectively, happily and self justifiably, I'm a free little nut or so it seems for I cannot escape the maniacal insanity that is my mind. In the few succeeding weeks I go on an exponentially intensified mind trip the likes of which would yield horrific results. My delusions of grandeur would go to the ultimate extremes. I now associate that Gerry has something of a hand in dropping the dime on me and go to the one person I haven't accused of such a self-perceived transgression, my younger sister's apartment. During that time I would come to a contemplative stance of such concepts as the bending of time, space and myself proclaimed dominion thereof, the ultimate assertion that I was God and conversely its disproval and supposed realization that there were aliens amongst us in more ways than imaginable.

The name of her apartment complex is Camelot, another sign via my reference through my self-administered education that is, "The Celestine Prophecy," authored by James Refield. Of course it's the gist of the thought, in my mind that is

insane in the membrane Germain who is actually
delusional even greater still Mihkalia, a blue ray
seraph, I was present during the reign of Author
at Avalon. But once again in my account that
is my own subjectively verified identity as the
crazy little Germain, I am at odds with Church
Triumphant's assertions as to my incarnational
lineage. I surmise I was and am, actually Gallahad
further justified by the vision in meditation of
myself as a knight lo all those years ago, while in
the thick of my "training." My mother is up from
Florida out of concern for my well-being and is
also staying at said apartment along with me and
my sister's roommate. I'm still playing music at
this point in time with the band I formed in the
spring of 2000, Break of Dawn. At this juncture
I start to entertain thoughts that this realm we
dwell in is actually the astral realm to which I
went in service after my sojourn of Sri Yuketswar
and not actually Terra, but that which I dub,
"Terra Incognita." In said realm I'm serving those
entities that are stuck here in the capacity of
freeing them from their limiting belief systems.

Then the insanity takes a turn toward paranoid
schizophrenia, through the impetus that is a
realization thought that even in this realm there
are aliens, of benevolent and bellicose nature,
among us. I petition the aid of Lucifer, a being I

now associate as likened unto a long lost loving
brother, and wage a battle versus "the grays",
within my psycho mind. We annihilate them
through the power of "our" angelic minds and
send them back to the void which is the existence
beyond the outer rim of the universe or the
unmanifest from which all possibilities and being
originate. It's now, through the practice of the
"Who knows" school of thought that I nearly
render myself catatonic. I take the ultimate stance
that was developing ; that is the entirety of the
universe operates via subjectivity and through
the assertion of the "Who knows" Socratic mind
twisted into my own subjective insanity that
ultimately comes for me the perceived objective
absolute that I AM GOD. I have now become
the ultimate creator of the insanity that is the
universe of my mind, or have I. The result of this
"realization" is the rendering of catatonia. All
is silent as the rearing cacophony in my mind
abates; "Holy Shit" I think "I'm the only one here
and I made this all up, it's all in my mind, I am
God. I am blown away to the point of awareness
that is completely detached and removed from
reality, approaching a point of no return. Then
through the counter attack that resurfaces, after
a time period that I am unaware of but that seems
infinite, of the thoroughly contradicted torment
that is my mind, I return. I'm staring around the

apartment totally catatonic and it hits me; I start laughing hysterically "I didn't make these walls," is the thought, and it continues "I didn't hang these cabinets, surely I am not God."

I go for a ride to get smokes and the jaunts which I've been "experiencing" all the while continue. I now start to reason through the faculties of my advancing insanity, that I unknowingly through the power of my self-proclaimed, self-perceived mind of God realization, am bending time and space, and am ultimately responsible for these dimensional jumps. It's another realization that strikes fear at my core for now I start to think of myself as a sort of Sam on Quantum Leap that is stuck in an unending series of dimensional jumps with no hope for return. Then it hits me, a light breaks through the night, "the medication anchors me in a time space reality." I rush home to Gerry at 3 AM and take medication, but ultimately my mind is not assuaged. I almost pass out into sleep while driving back to my sisters. By the grace of God I make it there and sleep for the first time in days.

Within a couple of days my sister has had enough for I am an unwelcome, uninvited guest so I petition my bass player for a place to stay for a couple of days. In his infinite kindness he welcomes me and I am off to his house in Patchogue. It's

there that I become aware of a perceived truth of
mind blowing proportions. While in his basement
playing with his dog something bizarre happens.
I see his dog, through the faculties of inner vision
as the reptilian race of aliens that I walked with,
so long ago, or such is my perception. They're a
most beautiful benevolent race here to assist us
in our development as our "best friends" is my
perception. At this time I also become aware
that SRF and Kirk are immersed in meditative
prayer to aid and further empower me and my
"pursuit." Then my mind twists and reels and I see
they are doing this for their own ends, a thirst for
world dominion. This is unacceptable to me and I
sever the mental connection with them and "view
and monitor" their collective unconscious from a
perspective of detachment. Currently, I begin to
entertain the thought via delusional grandiose
grandeurism, in memory of Captain Kirk's call
and reference to me that my "identity" while
not God is ultimately the next best thing. I am
actually Archangel Michael, prince of all heaven's
hosts. As previously stated; my ego knows no
bounds. Of course I "reason", Andrew, strong,
Michael my new identity meaning who is as God,
Lawless meaning both beyond the law of karma
that binds man; and angel and simultaneously the
absence of any karma, I am a field of untouched
snow. Ultimately, I reason, it's all been a mind

trip in which it was my destined role to fulfill prophecy through means of the critical mass of the collective unconscious. This is actually my first incarnation, I surmise, in which I have come to bear witness and through my experiences God will render final judgment on all humanity, such is now my delusional mission.

This, once again, is not the Andrew that's the sane little docile Andrew everybody loves, the proverbial dime is dropped once again; and you guessed it, following the yellow brick road courtesy of SCPD, I'm off to see the wizard that is USBH.

10
The Dark Night Goes Completely Black, Nearly

During this stay at Eastern Long Island Hospital, Greenport, I'm nearly broken. I say nearly for as I've said and say again in a case of redundancy, I'm a stubborn lil' ole mule, that saying bend or you break with a whole sicker twist on it, I'm bent to the point where I can neither be straightened nor broken. Many associations come to the fore again, redundancy, and I'm off to the races now redefined as a crazy motherfucking Archangel Michael literally from hell that was my stay in Brookhaven with Lucifer, and on a mission. This definition as you are now becoming to see was however still open to extrapolation. For at this time I consider the association that I am Michael of Nebanon, neba gone, as would be my delirium resurfacing as a ranting in Ebonics. "Of course" I muse, "it was actually James, not Jesus, that is this Michael of which was the seventh of my incarnations this now being my eighth with a psycho ninety degree twist on it that is representative of Infinity, a concept even mathematics has to reckon with, I am ultimately leading us home. "After all," I consider, "it's in *a little blue book, which through the Elizabeth Clare Prophets books represents the will of God while simultaneously subject to my now proclaimed means of discernment, arrived at through strict training of the best Yogic method available, it has to be true. "I laugh at myself seeing how tremendously thin that is, even to the psycho that is me and decide rather than the fact that I am crazy, no, I'm still the crazy motherfucking Archangel Michael whose base station is on earth home taking a little looksee in on what's happening and doing some house cleaning in the form of ridding us of the malicious mind processing Universal Scum. Yea, Yea that's it! But that's simply not good enough to pacify my ego, for now I make the association that I am Michael referenced in Judaism, Christianity and Islam all of which I come to see as mere platitudes and jump the remaining perceived gap to I am represented in the pantheonic Hinduism as Indra, which I render ultimately a monotheism via associating Brahma as the father of us all. While this is all well and good it is still not good enough and I toy with the possibility of being one of the original gods referred to in Zacharia Stitchin's books of speculation which I kicked around at Brookhaven. Now with most bases secure and some still open for definition I take the mind trip into overdrive after all is* it apparent I can't drive 55, at least not in my mind and go into "speculatory contemplative" mode in order to associate and define myself as Lord Michael. During this psychotic rumination I consider the possibility of parallel lives, the division of consciousness to achieve these ends and the nature of higher self if it be relevant in as much as anything being higher. I consider the arch typical versus the completely uniquely imbued. I came to the "knowledge "that I have indeed lived many lives at critical junctures of historical relevance but am usually not the main player but got honorable mention as one of the supporting ensemble. Of course, James, and now Ananda, and Arjuna, all my incarnations of Archangel Michael, it is at this time that I completely sever ties with the notion that I am the insane in the membrane Germain, in favor of this, what I perceive to be, ultimate angelic awareness. I consider the fact that Germain has actually been made up, a fictional character, but then remember the "historic accounts" of the man of that name and ultimately decide he's real, being none other than my brother Daniel. "Of course," is the logic, "he simply walked into me awakening my awareness." But he's a crazy little Germain and I warn him to keep his distance lest he drive me mad again. Which is a statement of epic irony; considering my insane mindset! And so now I

adopt the extrapolation, that this indeed is the
Revelations, as this is the 4th seal, I am opening,
as crazy motherfucking Archangel Michael,
which as all the seals have been symbolized by
the correlating stays in the hospitals. Now it's air
tight, the justifying of the flourishing of insanity.
Still with me? I am Clint Westwood, the Pale
Rider. But let's not get ahead of ourselves; back to
the associations.

In now what is a case of redundant redundancy,
through means of myself administered education,
through faculties of discernment cultivated via
training in the purported best yogic means of
realization available, I make many associations of
both staff and patients through what I reiterate
is the total insanity that is my mania. My mother
I now associate is actually my little sister Ruth
from my life as James the Just, my older sister
is actually Martha of Bethany and my friend is
actually Hagar, who was then my mother in the
life that is my dawning awareness as Ismail, son
of Abraham. She's still like a lost abandoned child
is the reference through a patient. "Mary, Mary,
quite contrary, trim that bush it's so dam hairy."
Oh! The beat goes on; Morya, Lucifer, Buddha
and Saul are also represented through said
associations. It's now that I go on to contemplate
the nature of conflict. Is it man against nature,

man against man and man against himself
as purported in literary intellectualism, via
dissemination by Mrs. Muller all those years
ago? "No," I surmise it all is metaphoric of that
which is man against himself," is the nature of
the "realization." Then it happens, something that
still strikes fear in me to this very day. While
exercising #6 in The Patient's Bill of Rights, I'm
denied smoking privileges. I petition my attorney
Bob Day and inform him that via a religious
observance which is my affiliation with said habit,
by means of Shamanism, my right to freedom of
religion, smoking is a sacred practice thereof and
cannot be denied me. The staff is informed such by
said attorney and relent to the degree of taking
me to the cage and back for smokes after the
other patients have completed said privilege. The
stage is set for Hell in every way. One particular
evening I am denied my smoke break and the shit
hits the fan in the form of me freaking out on the
head nurse. It ends with me stating, "Someone
get Day." Then thinking I'm actually threatening
their lives, code blue is called and I'm kindly out
in four points.

I would spend the next five days and succeeding
nights therein. The doctors come to me regularly
and inform me I'm not to be released from
restraints until I comply and take medications.

I fly off the handle from the predicament I'm in and state it's within my rights to refuse, afforded me via The Patient's Bill of Rights. To no avail but what's worse is that my behavior is justifying their method. On the second night I start to leave my body, or so it seems for I'm so doped up by the regular injections being administered at the behest of Dr. Slugger. This is not a pleasurable sensation however for ultimately I "return" to my body and the shackled state I find myself in. It's complete hell and on the third day I relent, concede and take medication in hopes of escaping this very real hell.

It's off to court once more for even in my compliance I'm a little nut who can't be trusted and they get Kendra's Law once again, even referencing the fact that I had to be restrained for an extended period of time, thusly justifying the threat that is me. Six more month's mandatory medications, is the result.

11
Good and Compliant Boy
Interrupted

The treatment plan consists of lithium citrate, Seroquel, a weekly hour long session with Dr. Chuang, weekly half hour therapy session with Reverend Heffler and an occasional visit or session with the Act team, and monthly blood tests to both monitor and affirm the medications' presence. I follow reluctantly until something totally unforeseen happens, my mania overtakes the medication. It starts with a dream of my Dad in which his head turns into that of the Buddha. It's further justification to my insanity in the form of a clearer "realization" that my father was in fact the Buddha and I am none other than the venerable Ananda, which initially dawned on me while at Brookhaven. Eventually, though at this point in time compliant, it dawns on me the medication is of no use and is ultimately a prolonged death sentence through contraindications. I miss my doctor's appointment, am paid a visit by the Act team and it's off to see the Wizard once more.

This would be the first of two successive stays at Stony Brook, the former of which would prove to be quite hilarious. I'm in psycho Archangel Michael mode with a wry twist that is the humor in stereotypes. I consider the jaded perspective of police officers, through the references of memories of my father, and come to see the relevant truth and subsequent hilarity in it. I dubbed myself smart cop and my partner Lucifer, who I now associate as John Lennon, the re-embodiment of John the Baptist or as I refer to him "El Baptismo", dumb cop. I was James and he John is the "reasoning", Michael and Lucifer. At this time the God I'm praying to keeps on getting me locked up so I come up with the idea that I should petition Mel Brooks to write me out of this scenario. Ultimately hysterical delirium ensues in what is now my total state of mania. I get the feeling we were all pot heads in those days of Christ and a play-like scene equipped with dialog ensues that is a vision of me as James. "Hey John," I say. "Hey James," he replies. "I've got some Roman Red John, I can't smoke that shit anymore James every time I do I think God's talking to me," he states. "Wow John, you're going to lose your head," I say. "What about you James?" he questions. "You know me John, "I say, "I love getting stoned." "Here comes Jesus", he says, "my brother is such a pain in the ass" I say, "he's always hanging around, I wish he would die but he'd probably just come back to haunt me." The hilarity continues for I *think of John's prophecies of doom in those days when Jesus came as the great redeemer and his apparent subsequent message of, "Give Peace a Chance," in this now the time I've come to dub the Revelations, he's most definitely "dumb cop" I laugh hysterically. Ultimately to make and exceedingly long story, with a recurring theme, short; I don't even bother going to the court trial and am now under Kendra's Law for a year from release.*

12
The First Rays of Dawn

During the next year I am compliant without
a hitch and continue to read of spirit, now with
the hopes of realization but rather with the hopes
of being saved from this madness somehow. I
continue to write music and find a grounding
therein. I read of Maitreya and his masters and
how this is the time of their great gathering
and thusly begin to petition him with prayer
in hopes of somehow being healed. I learn of the
water pills associated with this, "master," and
Gerry acquires them, while I secretly hope they
will cure me of bi-polar disorder. The years go by
and I begin to seek alternative treatment in the
form of acupuncture. This is the beginning of the
repetitive cycle of madness. I ultimately go off
medication secretly against the urging of doctors,
Gerry and my family and I'm on the prowl once
more with a renewed and intensified vigor.
During this time I revisit the association that my
father was the Buddha and I Ananda. I write
the entirety of a journal of supposed, apparent
or imagined memories and communications with
daddy Buddha but ultimately burn it out of fear
of reprisal. That simply however cannot contain

or pacify what by now you should well see is; the insanity of my ego; I'm the big bad Id.

Gerry and I have an argument, she knows I'm going manic and doesn't know what to do being well aware of the fact that I entertained thoughts of suicide after my stay at Eastern. She was the one who nursed and ultimately brought me back. I'm driving in my car, as the song goes and engaged in the "balancing" of the self-perceived collective unconscious, when I run out of gas. I'm on the LIE westbound about a quarter of a mile east of exit 48 or Round Swamp Road, Plainview. It's no problem though I know the area from it being my route at Columbia Courier for years and figure I'll walk up to the gas station on the corner of the south service road and get a tank and some gas. What happens next is something of a walk through the dimensional jaunts, via the bending of time and space manifestations that are, the corridors in the crazy little universe that is my mind. I'd be gone for almost a whole day and eventually walk back to Lindenhurst and get a ride home from a friend. There's no more blackness that envelopes me in these perceived jaunts, for apparently I've advanced to some degree, rather now they have the effect of a slight manipulative disturbance likened unto heat rising off the street on a hot summer's day. I get the

tank and gas and return to my car but by this
time I'm so cold that I can't manage to get the
gas in my car and have to seek shelter within it
from the elements. Maybe there's something to
that man against nature I think, but ultimately
annihilate that through my "angelic buddhic
mind that was Annanda, " in consideration of
"no hot, no cold, " indicative of the boddhisatvic
mind-set. As night recedes in its everyday cycle
of destruction that is the birth of dawn I return
to Round Swamp Road and consider in another
example of contemplative psychosis, the nature of
mathematics and Newtonian physics as opposed
to that of the newly emerging Quantum Theory.
Ultimately I see how completely ridiculous they
are and render them arbitrary assignations of
that which simply stated IS. In this rumination I
dub myself, "Andy to the Infinity minus 1 power;
less than but not quite equal to God while rapidly
approaching said domain through a tangential
graph type representation with the ultimate goal
of supplanting said god and establishing dominion
for myself as such." Not seriously, for at this
point in time I'm a happy, nutty, little Archangel
Michael, or am I ultimately through the quantum
phenomena that is; the observer and observational
energy thusly generating the observed. This then
I render a steaming pile of horseshit though,
referencing the life of William Shakespeare that

is the insane in the membrane Germain, now as
previously stated my brother Daniel asserting
via the rose that which is simply independent of
our attributal assignations in search of defined
meaning. Greater than or equal to if and only if
then or and . . . goes the spinning of mathematics
in my head that I assess is man's continuing, ever
adjusting, attempts at knowledge with the goal of
being able to sleep at night secure in the notion
the sky won't fall or such is the perception. In
my mind I then see the memory of meditation
all those years ago and my supposed missing link
between Newtonian and Quantum physics that
has its basis in basic wave theory the Unified
Theory that Einstein sought.

With that I get up and hit the universal Mobile
for some smokes. Now I start to put a spin
on "Andy to the infinity minus 1 power," and
reconsider the Indra association. In correlation
with the crazy Archangel Michael theory and
redefine myself via Dungeons and Dragons
reference, "little, itty, witty bitty, most merciful/
vengeful demigod lil' ole me, worship me!" and
with that I am laughing hysterically again fully
aware of how insane I am, while as Loverboy
put it am, "loving every minute of it." In these
jaunts I travel a scope of our solar system,
that is to say apparently, for in my insanity

comes the first hint of its limitation; I have no
knowledge of reference beyond that. I further
work on and consider the purposeful of bending
of time and space. I travel to Jupiter and hang
with the "Jupitans," as I dub them in Amityville.
Amityville on Jupiter is a clean and beautiful
town where it becomes apparent that there is
no tolerance for the street walking trash that is
"little, itty, witty bitty, most merciful/vengeful
demigod lil' ole me". An unmarked cruiser pulls
up and the cop inside is quite animated in his
assertion that he doesn't care where I go as long as
I get the hell out of dodge. When he pulls away, I
perceive myself to bend time and space and send
him to Pluto, via my angelic mind where he will
wander aimlessly in search of me futilely for I on
Jupiter with the jupitans. "Worship me," I project
to his mind, "calling car five, calling car five go
to Uranus," is the delirious continuance of the
perceived projection through utter insanity. It's
now through my faculties of dominion over the
illusion which is time and space that I practice,
to paraphrase the Frank Zappa school of thought,
referenced from his Phase One disc, the sending of
bad little boys to stay on E or as I term it; beyond
the outer rim. For now as you can see, only barely
if at all serious now in a total state of delirium,
I'm a "most merciful/vengeful little, itty, witty
bitty, demigod lil' ole me; worship me. While this

is all well and fine, I'm out of money, smokes and
am freezing for apparently it is a little colder
on Jupiter. I start walking home down Sunrise
Highway and stop into a porn shop to get warm.
It's here that I have a most profound insight into
homosexuality. I see the covers to the movies as all
men and women, even the gay titles and "reason
that the body and identification of sex are but
an illusion and ultimately any act of love be it
"gay or straight" is beautiful and to be celebrated.
After all I'm a crazy motherfucking Archangel
Michael who is ultimately androgynous.

In the end case scenario, I make it to Lindenhurst,
where my buddy is working and ask for a ride
home. He brings me to my older sister's house
where my mother is again present, having gotten
on a flight while they were looking on earth
for me, while the majority of the time I was on
Jupiter. They eventually drop the dime and I am
off once again to see the wizard of Id.

13
The Healing Begins

This is the later of my aforementioned stays at Stony Brook and is the last stop on this mystery tour that is at least to date. Ultimately it proves to be my surrender and the end to the war that I have waged for several years now within my mind. I'm sitting in my room in the psych ward and it comes to me in a flash:

"of course, I instantly come to realize through the means of signs," which I would come to realize was the self-created universe that existed in my mind, to the awareness via the buddhic mind of that which was my infinitely varied lineage which was arrived at via associative patterns correlative to my self-administered educational references, via my developed faculties of discernment, that ultimately matters not through the mind only perspective in which all is the extension of the one mind referenced in redundancy through the Jeshua Letters and subsequently it's annihilation by means of A Course in Miracles where the ego is the dissident of truth and perpetrator of illusions continuance through a means of detachment from that which we call reality, arrived at through non-violent resistance via Mohandas Gandhi, adherent to a high authority, and then the ultimate surrender to the will of God or Tao which is the one true reality." It comes to me in a picture the resolution to the war which has waged within my mind to which the wars of the outward world seem insignificant, I see St. John's, the injections, IM or I am I remember the time space anchor being the medication and the ultimate torture that was the code blue or the will of God, at Greenport, it hits me square in the face. This God's will for me all along I've been praying for a life line and this is it. These people, my brothers and sisters, are trying to help me. I comply with their treatment plan and accept their diagnosis. The battle is won, what you resist persists. I am released within two weeks, the shortest of all my stays.

14
Two Feet on the Ground

That was approximately three years ago now and from then up to present I've been in a state of accepting compliance by means of a very real Earth Angel in the form of Nurse Practitioner Susan Akin. She actually listens to what I say and we ultimately tackle this thing together working with specifics of levels of medications so I can still have some form of cognizance and enjoy a rewarding and fulfilling life all the while keeping two feet on the ground.

My family and friends have returned to me and are happy with the sane docile little Andrew while if I must be completely honest with you, there is a part of me that has yet to return. Some times at night when Gerry and the dogs are sleeping I light a cigarette and think about all of it trying to decipher what if any meaning there was and is in all of it. On one particular evening it started as usual, "Insanity or Epiphany" I mused as that thought echoed in repetition across my mind. Then with the dawning of a warm feeling I think of my brother Danny and slowly as if waking from a sleep it dawns on me, a thought, Illusory.

I think of the Jeshua Letters which I have read several times it's all a dream and with that thought starts the music in my head, it's a song I wrote entitled "It's Just a Dream." The lyrics are as follows:

> *And I finally see*
> *What goes on goes on inside me ?*
> *Well I've seen the light and*
> *I've walked through darkest night*
> *It's just a dream and I'm dreaming life again.*

> *Well I woke with a start and silence filled the dark*
> *Then just one thought came to me*
> *What if I dream, what I be and everything I see*
> *Could this just all be a dream?*
> *Inside of me lies the stirring of deep memories*
> *And now I think . . . that I*

> *Finally see*
> *What goes on goes on inside me.*
> *Well I've seen the light and*
> *I've walked through darkest night*

It's just a dream and I'm dreaming life
again.

Then it turns me around,
When it all comes crashing down
Reality calls to me
Then a thought breaks free,
It's the challenge of the dream
Still I just don't know what to believe
It's all puzzling yet surrealistic I can see
These unfolding scenes

And I can finally see
What goes on goes on inside me
Well I've seen the light and
I've walked through darkest night
It's just a dream and I'm dreaming life
again.

Guitar Solo

Sometimes you win, sometimes you lose
Sometimes you sing the Blues
Sometimes you're up, sometimes you're down
Sometimes it turns you 'round
Feeling good, feeling bad
You're happy then you're sad
Alive and well, sick as hell
I've stood and I have fell

Wound tight; then you're loose
  You're sober then you're juiced
Can't miss, can't hit
Sometimes it's all bullshit!

And I finally see
  What goes on goes on inside me
   Well I've seen the light and
    I've walked through darkest night
   It's just a dream and I'm dreaming
life again.

  Repeat into subsequent fade

Then my awareness returns to the room with a
sense of inquisitive peace, illusionary, a dream I
consider, but what is real? And with that thought
the music starts again only this time it's "On the
found way," which lyrically follows:

  Do I wake? what's this trap door built
  within my gaze
  On the lake, what's this reason, what's
  it we've made?
  Still I breathe, still I bathe in all this I
  embrace
  What I feel I can't say they'll all lock
  me away.

*And what is real I ask myself this
everyday
Unasked questions, they just burn my
mind away
          On the found way.*

*Wandering amid illusions, my bow
steers away
Listening, as we cut down each other
each day
This imagery, this mass confusion it
blows me away
I feel myself slipping out now, I don't
know what to say*

*And what is real I ask myself this
every day
Unasked questions they just blow my
mind away
          On the found way*

But ultimately the question still begging to be
asked is, "what is real?' The wheels start turning
again and at the risk of going insane I surrender
via an affirmation I coined early on in my
insanity that is, "I don't know and I don't care I'm
wearing God's underwear," and in that moment
I lay back and look at the ceiling as I offer that

which I grab hold of as my final thought on the matter which keeps me secure in the notion that the sky won't fall on me, which is; "assholes abound and it starts from within!" and thusly I drift off to sleep.

15
A Glimpse into the Ultimate Mind-fucker that is Me

The preceding chapter could very well have been a good enough ending but does not assuage or render justice to the egomaniac to end all that I am, so fasten your seatbelts while I endeavor to take you on a ride into the ultimate mind-fucker that is me. I'll start slow with a sonnet:

I come as a brother
Seems there be something in a name
On a quest to find truth
Even if I go insane
No life, no death
Not within this illusionary game
I seek not to purport
I've no concern for personal gain
The ultimate goal now peace
Escape from the cacophony; a refrain
'Tis there I make my abode
'Tis there I shall remain
The Grand Master of Racozky
Captain Insano
Saint Germain

And thusly continue with a Nostradamic like
Quatrain

All is well
Even with Lucifer in hell as far as I can tell
Worship me
I am Lord Michael

Of Nebanon perhaps
Neba no

Adieu, a big reeking pile of horseshit!

I A.M. Lawless
Public psycho #1

"Memories of a past engender that which is fear
Is it of the ego, as to truth I draw near
I sever ties to outcomes and placidity overcomes me
'Tis there I find the resolution to the search for peace
'Tis there I am free."

For to state the ultimate assertion of truth that
abides in peace;
"I am Incarnito, the incognito incarnation, known
not even to self, rather only to God; unless not,
who knows?

"Who knows? unless not,
Unless not, who knows?

That is to say who knows, maybe none of us; unless
not, which is to say I might know; Unless not,
which is to say I don't know; who knows? That is
to say maybe I actually do! On ad infinitum, and
with this thought I am reminded of the song I
wrote with Gerry entitled appropriately enough
"Truth?" the punctuation being intended. The
lyrics are as follows:

> *Struggling, against the why?*
> *My intentions confused*
> *Into the abyss my mind does spy*
> *Searching for some clues*
>
> *Beyond the fringe of the rational mind*
> *Walking the wire behind the time*
> *I turn away from the collective jive*
> *But the fear always seeks to bind*
>
> *What kind of price does one have to pay?*
> *What if it's true?*
> *When questions run too deep*
> *What's scaring you?*
> *Who really knows anything?*
> *Maybe, not you?*
> *Do I shake your precious truth?*

In this dungeon of your compromise
You paint your thoughts on me
And now this label above my eyes
Never again to be free

I take your burden
I wear your guilt
Of your ignorance I've had my fill
But you can't change what's beyond
your will
No shot, no shame, no shackle, no pain
not even a pill

What kind of price does one have to pay?
What if it's true?
When questions run too deep
What's scaring you?
Who really knows anything?
Maybe not you
Did I shake your precious truth?

SOLO BREAK

Beyond the fringe of the rational mind
Walking the wire behind the time
I turn away from the collective jive
But the fear always seeks to bind

What kind of price does one have to pay?

What if it's true?
When questions run too deep
What's scaring you?
Who really knows anything?
Maybe not you did I shake your
precious truth?

"Who knows, unless not;
Unless not, who knows . . ."
On ad infinitum

"They were right putting that fucker Socrates to
death, he corrupted all of our minds, he fucked us."

"Who knows, unless not;
Unless not, who knows . . ."
Therefore . . . who cares."

The ultimate stance from which all that is pure
potentially arises. The ultimate dualistic altruism;
the Mobius Loop, omega, the end!

Take that Socrates, fuck you very much!

And now it's onward and upward to the next
witch hunt; is the means ultimately the end or
does the end justify the means; look out

Machiavelli, your psychosis is thin at best next to mine, here I come you fucker!

Or is ultimately the means the end, through diligent practice and repetition brings about desired creational results? Maybe I'm not the sickest fucker of them all and maybe I am, who knows? unless not; unless not, who knows? Is Neale really talking to God or am I talking to him? Christomaniacs of the world unite. I still got it! What the heck it's the halo deck Gene."

Picard Out!

"Seek not to purport via self-destructive means, I'm nobody's fucking patsy, not even God's. Fuck you Father, thy will be done, for in the words of the goddess Santa Monica Blvd., all I wanna do is have some fun."

"I got my six pack and my guitar, just lying low Got no means, got no reason, got nowhere to go . . ."
    A.M. Lawless from "wasting time"

p.s.
"pee, pee, in your pants, like that which we are, warring little ants."

Peace
Amen
A man
Unless not, who knows?
Maybe
Perhaps
Possibility
Potentially
Relatively
Kinetically
A man
Human?
Huh?, mann!
"Who knows, therefore who cares"

Chillin" like Dylan, peace out, word to yo mutha,
I'm a cowboy baby, we're all nineteen years old,
or at least were at one point, baby please don't go.
I'm a voodoo chile', your hoochie coochie man, . . .
and on and on . . . anon-da!

Thespus

"Denny Crane; still undefeated!"
        - Captain Kirk

Assholes abound and it starts from within
        - Incarnito

101

Bengay
How long?
Homosexual
Homosapian?
Homo ape eon?
Bisexual?
Bipolar
Night and day
Who knows?
Unless not
The chicken
Or the egg
A-sexual?
A sexual mother fucker!
Once upon a time
Not so long after then
Yesterday
Before tomorrow
After past
Prior to future
So long ago
What is and what never shall be
Identity!
One!!!!!

Unless not, who knows?
Descartes I think Socrates doth live! Unless not!
I think therefore I am nuts
The ancient Astronaut

God is dead
We are the superman
Be wary of kryptonite
Lest you go insane
In the membrane
Within the game
That never was
So says el cuz
Who on Earth do you think you are?
A superstar
Well right you are!
Blacker than night, a soul brother inside out
A real nigga I doth espout
A player pimps and ho's
Who knows
Unless not
Booger snot
I bet you a hundred the Smells kid eats it
Utterly insane, a tit
A master
An angel
A devil
A ghost
An embodiment of the comforter?
An ascended host?
A holy roller rockin' on
Hailing from the great big psycho farm!
From whence I came
Yet always did remain

Best I now can tell Earth
For what it's worth
Quick Robin, to the bat cave
Gotham we must save
USA, new Rome?
The big apple I call home
My satanic temptative insanity
Though most often enough harmlessly
 So fuckin' what
 Love is smut
 King fuckin' Tut
 I'm most obviously a fuckin' nut
 The chicken or the egg
 Alright, end it now I sense you beg?
 I won't acquiesce
 At you bequest
 I'll continue on Anon, anon-da
 Well fuck you, go to hell
 To me it's just as well
 3 cigs per break
 Oh! For hell's sake
 Get to hang with bros
 Through down Socratic pros
 We are birds of a feather
 Us nuts that run together
 So get on the bus
 Remember the Master, don't judge us
 It's a movie
 A big game

Take it lightly
Lest here you remain
And what of free will?
Was not mine to swallow the pill
Make not a mountain out of a mole hill
Lest you eventually take ill
Was I born
Prior to this sojourn
Before then less than but not quite equal
to and infinitely approaching now
Wow, tao, kapow!
Do we have to die
Seems silly, I wonder why
No, death is but a door
To forever more, my Eleanor
And to say it again ultimately who
knows?
And so on the insanity goes
Not anymore!
Who cares!
Come back down now children
There, there . . .

"if I don't meet you no more in this world,
I'll meet you in the next one . . . don't be; late;
maybe?"

And so now it ends with my greatest teacher,
the love of all my lives, that as far as I can tell is

this one; whose unwavering faith in me gives me the only meaning I could possibly think of in the master's teachings that thus states. "Verily I say unto you a man must be born anew to enter the kingdom," I get it; you are eternal beauty that engenders my life every time I look into your eyes.

Gerry, my love once asked me
Who are you?"
"An angel of mercy," was my response
"But you're not saying who you really think you are," she says lovingly with a most beautiful smile. "It's alright, you'll spend the rest of your life not knowing and all of eternity finding out!"

Gerry
My immortal beloved, my twin flame; . . . Goddess

"thank you"
        - Led Zeppelin

Incarnito, the psycho-thespian over stated and ultimately out . . . of my mind!

16
Warning! Don't try this at Home You Must be a Good and Well-trained Psycho

For Dad and Danny,
>Daddy Buddha and insane in the
>membrane
>Thanks for showing me the way;
>Until we meet again . . .
>I'll see you in my dreams or maybe not
>. . . who knows?
>I love you!

>"The Gambler"
>-Kenny Rogers

Less than but not quite equal to and rapidly approaching God only knows;
>And I am most assuredly "not it."

Most merciful/vengeful little, itty, witty bitty lil' ole me demigod;
>Andy is the infinity minus one power!

"it has been undone!"
"not it"
Tautology!

"is the glass half full or half empty;
The chicken or the egg?"
Mathematical union
True or false=true
True or true=true
False or true=true
False or false=true
Neither-One!!!!!!!!!!
Tautology

17
File Reopened

This book was written in majority over Easter weekend 2006, with finishing brush strokes added in the days that followed. I've never considered entering the forum of authorship but like John said to Sean, "life is what happens to you while you're making other plans." It is now approaching the better part of a decade later and there have been seven subsequent hospitalizations, from 2007 to 2012, with many perceived satori's of enlightening experiences, or may have not, that's fuel for fodder of a second manuscript. I had started in the following months of this books completion. I had always thought music was my destined purpose, who knows?, unless not, who knows?

These days I find solace in the applications of the theosophical studies and applications therein. Maybe I'll finish that manuscript titled "<u>Roofing, Siding and Modern Mysticism; with a Touch of Crazy.</u>" I've kept a great deal of journals of poetry, "realizations and teachings." Everybody loves the Trinity so I figure, "What the fuck, maybe I'll go that route." I did start that and as well titled, "<u>Prose of the Dreamer and the Dream.</u>" Who

knows? *Unless not, Insanity, Epiphany, Illusory;*
Who knows?, unless not, unless not, who knows?

Andrew

Cold Day

Wait for my season to change
Soon, time in my hands
Secrets made open the door and fly
away.

Sleep, peaceful dreams to keep
Breathe, life I come to know
From the ashes I lift myself back home.

Feel the breeze caress my dreams
Free at last or so it seems
Winged arms carry me away
Carry me away.

Seek, test the water, my friend
Believe. In the means and not the end
It's a cold, cold day
From where I've been.

Solo

Wait, for my season to change
Soon, time in my hands
It's a cold, cold day from where I've been
Cold day. (4 times)

Is That All

And in my fueled escape the tanks are
Burning out
The Shore light fades away, darkness
Creeping down.
The mist of common place
Wraps itself around
I wrestle in the grasp of
Nothing to be found
And then the war parade filters
Through the ground and they
Poison the pure waters until we all
drown
Is that all
The children gather and play
One day to lay claim and slay
This power laden crusade
Dictates every move we make
When will the peace reign
And minds act from love again
Amid the mist we made
Blinded to a better way
And then the war parade . . .

Solo

And still these wars we wage
When will they find the way
This information age
We forge onto the grave
Amid this mist we wade
Blinded to a better way

When will the peace reign
Is that all (4 times)

Truth

Struggling, against the why?
My intentions confused
Into the abyss my mind does spy
Searching for some clues

Beyond the fringe of the rational mind
Walking the wire behind the time
I turn away from the collective jive
But the fear always seeks to bind

What kind of price does one have to
pay?
What if it's true?
When questions run too deep
What's scaring you?
Who really knows anything?
Maybe not you?
Do I shake your precious truth?

In this dungeon of your compromise
You paint your thoughts on me
And now this label above my eyes
Never again to be free

I take your burden
I wear your guilt
Of your ignorance I've had my fill

But you can't change what's beyond
your will
No shot, no shame, no shackle, no pain
not even a pill

What kind of price does one have to
pay?
What if it's true?
When questions run too deep
What's scaring you?
Who really knows anything?
Maybe not you
Did I shake your precious truth?

SOLO BREAK

Beyond the fringe of the rational mind
Walking the wire behind the time
I turn away from the collective jive
But the fear always seeks to bind

What kind of price does one have to pay?
What if it's true?
When questions run too deep
What's scaring you?
Who really knows anything?
Maybe not you
Did I shake your precious truth?

Miriam

What is this that keeps me
    From you my love
Sickened in my healing ways
    I dream your touch
Longing to caress your hair
    And kiss your cheek
But the whispers in the wind
    They carry me
    Far from you my Miriam
    Forgive me my love.

In my mind I see the tear
    Form in your eye
Never falling, never yielding
    What's inside
Deepest love tendered with pain
    Of what must be
Missing your touch on this road
    That's called for me
    Far from you my Miriam
    Forgive me my love.

Pray for me
    Our Love to be my guide

Solo

What is this that keeps me
From you my love
Sickened in my healing ways
I dream your touch
Longing to caress your hair
And kiss your cheek
But the whispers in the wind
They carry me
Far from you my Miriam
Forgive me my love
I miss you my Miriam
Forgive me my love.

Drift It Away

Could this be all that I
    Have hoped for
Could you be my lover and
    So much more
Lay me down my baby in
    Ocean sands
Walk with me my lover
    Hand in hand
We'll drift it away and sail the
    Seven Seas
Just you and me my baby that's
    All we need

    We'll drift it away
    We'll drift it away
    We'll drift it away
    We'll drift it away

Tropical islands and ocean shores
    Just you and me in love
      Forever more
White capped mountains and a
    Deep blue sky
We'll spread our wings my baby
    Our love will fly

We'll drift it away and sail the
		Seven Seas

Just you and me my baby that's
		All we need

		We'll drift it away
		We'll drift it away
		We'll drift it away
		We'll drift it away

You're my freedom
		You're my mystery
Just you and me my Babe
		That's all we need
				Yeah! Yeah!

Could this be all that I
		Have hoped for
Could you be my lover and
		So much more
Lay me down my Baby in
		Ocean sands
Walk with me my lover
		Hand in hand

We'll drift it away and sail the
     Seven Seas
Just you and me my Baby
     That's all we need.

We'll drift it away
    We'll drift it away
    We'll drift it away
    We'll drift it away

One Shot

I sit and wait, and anticipate
 The right time to come
Bide my time, waitin' to align
 These feelings just begun
Smoothin' out the cracks
 Of our love undone
Walkin' back, across the facts
 Of this hit and run

Memories, shroud and hide
 All that we've been through
Wondering, just how and why
 I ever got involved with you
 And while I do.

One shot, just clouds my mind
 Two shots it comes undone
Three times and I leave my soul behind
 Thinking you were the one
I guess we had our fun

Wasted, walking on the bend
 And you with your man
Seems 'bout all I can do

Tryin' to understand
Hot went cold and sweet got old
It's all lost on me
Pour back another tryin' to arrange
One last final plea

It ain't no good and I know I should
Turn and walk away
But all that time still clouds my mind
So what's this price I have to pay

One shot, just clouds my mind
Two shots it comes undone
Three times and I leave my soul behind
Thinking you were the one
I guess we had our fun

Endless days walking through this haze
That reeks of you
'bout high time that I realize
All that crazy shit is thru

I cry Lord please save my soul
It's seems hell's come of me
Take this thirst, lift this curse
I cry, set me free

That hurtful woman cut down deep
  And now I'm drowning slow
Not quite sure what to do
  But I know this has got to go

Waiting on the lightning strike
  But all that I can see
Is the way that woman
  Has gotten the best of me.

One shot, just clouds my mind
  Two shots it comes undone
Three times and I leave my soul behind
  Thinking you were the one
I guess we had our fun

In the Seem

Will you speak or silence me
        Silence me with your mystery
I can see you're listening
        Hearing what is left unsaid
Uncertainty is circling where I breathe
        Ambiguity unsettling sanity,
        everything

Waiting for the sign I need
        Sign I need to direct me
Wondering just where I stand
        Sitting in this no man's land

In the middle of something I can't see
Where the lines are drawn is
        Lost on me . . . I can't see

In the seem I find, deep complexity
        Unknowing mind, in between
        down in the seem

Lines fade and I see my chance slip
away
Got to move but I just don't know
which way

Don't know how you feel; just don't
know what to say

No one to steer me and I see my chance
slip away

Will you speak or silence me
        Silence me with your mystery
I can see you're listening
        Hearing what is left unsaid

Uncertainty is circling, where I
breathe
Ambiguity unsettling sanity,
everything

In the seem I find deep complexity
Unknowing mind, in between down in
the seem
In the seem I find deep complexity
Unknowing mind, in between down in
the seem

        Where nothing is what it seems
        Feels just like a dream
        In between down in the seem.

Need

I want to tell you baby
Just how I feel
Want you to know it
Gotta make you see
Symbols are flowing
Landscapes are dusk
I crave your lovin'
Give it to me

Wasting away into a pool of my need
Hungering for your touch on me

Fire burns inside me
It's you that I need
This whimpering, lusting
Your love can heal
Why are you lying
When you say you don't want me
I sit here crying, crying in my need

Wasting away into a pool of my need
Hungering for your touch on me

This waiting game
Is killing me
Waiting here
In my need

Solo

Wasting away into a pool of my need
Hungering for your touch on me

I want to tell you baby
Just how I feel
Want you to know it
Gotta make you see
Symbols are flowing
Landscapes are dusk
I crave your lovin'
Give it to me

Wasting away into a pool of my need
Hungering for your touch on me

In Sin

I can't say, what I don't know
    Cutting away, time to let go
Will I pay for the things that I do
    I won't say, that I think that it's true
Darkness falls on my day

In sin, in sin, living in sin

Outrageous, are those claims that I hear
    Contagious, is the spread of the fear
Love sanctioned, is no greater to me
    I believe in a love that's free
Dogma casts down its grey

In sin, in sin, living in sin

Downcast thoughts come my way
Always somethin' to say

Solo

I can't say, what I don't know
    Cutting away, time to let go

Will I pay for the thing that I do
*   I won't say, that I think that it's true*
Darkness falls in my day

In sin, in sin, living in sin
In sin, in sin, living in sin

Weather Channel

I can't stand the rain
    Makes me go nuts
My ends all fray
    Smoke a lot of butts
I can't stand this place
    Turns me around
Gotta get away
    I scream out loud
It keeps on rainin' rainin' all damn day
    Waiting for a break to come so I
    can get away

This fuckin' heat
    Is killin' me
My brain feels like toast
    I wish it would freeze
Sweat burns my eyes
    I smell like shit
No big surprise
    I'm burnin' in it

It just keeps searin' searin'
    Me to the bone
I wish this heat would just leave me alone

It gets so cold that I can't take it
no more
What the fuck does it have
To get so cold for

Solo

I freeze my ass off, ass off all damn day
Working outside this weather is
drivin' me insane

Leaves falling down
What the fuck's the deal
Cleanin' this shit up
Is fuckin' unreal
Can't get no where
Keeps on coming down
Workin' all day
Like some fucking clown

It keeps on changing, changing every day
Working outside this weather
Is drivin' me insane

I'm to Blame

Well I can feel it comin'
    But I just can't see
Just where it's comin' from
    And what it means
Time is ripe for a change
    And I think I might be one
Tired of livin' my life baby
    Underneath you gun

Got to leave you now
Can't you see that things just
    Aren't the same
Got to leave you now and
I'm sorry to say
    I'm to blame

Well I'm sorry babe
    But I just don't love you the same
And you know I'm no good
    At playin' the pretend game
Things don't feel the same when
    You hold me in your arms
And it gets me to thinkin'
    That just might be my alarm
Got to leave you now

Can't you see that things just
    Aren't the same
Got to leave you now and
I'm sorry to say
    I'm to blame

Well I can feel it comin'
    But I just can't see
Just where it's comin' from
    And what it means
Time is ripe for a change
    And I think I might be one
Tired of livin' my life baby
    Underneath you gun

Got to leave you now
Can't you see that things just
    Aren't the same
Got to leave you now and
I'm sorry to say
    I'm to blame

Look for Andrew Lawless
"Break of Dawn 27" on iTunes.

Bibliographical References

The I Am discourses by Godfre Ray King
Saint Germain: on the Adept in the Aquarian Age
Elizabeth Claire Prophet
Saint Germaine on Prophecy Elizabeth Claire
Prophet
Autobiography of a Yogi Paramahansa
Yogananda
The Holy Science Sri Yuketswar
Conversations with God bks. 1-3 Neale Donald
Walsch
Confucius the analects
Zen and the art of Motorcycle Maintenance
Robert Presig
Mirror of Conciosness Elizabeth Clare Prophet
The Baghavad Gita
The Koran
The teachings of the Buddha
The Dhamapada Narada
The Jeshua Letters Mark Harmmer
A Course in Miracles
Thus Spoke Zarathstra F Neitze
Illusions Richard Bach
A stranger in a strange land Robert A. Heinlen
The Last Scrolls of King Solomon
Bloodline of the Holy Grail

The Hiram Key
The P'taah tapes Jani King
The Seth books Jane Roberts
Whispers from Eternity Paramahansa Yogananda
The Keys to Enoch
The Urantia Book
The Bible old and New Testament
Angel Blessings Cards
The Ra Material an ancient astronaut speaks
Don Elkins, Carla Rueckert, and James Allen
McCarthy
The Yoga Sutras of Patanjali by Sri Swami
Satchidananda
The Great White Brotherhood by Elizabeth Clare
Prophet
The masters and Their Retreats Mark L. Prophet
and Elizabeth Clare Prophet
Socrates Buddha Confucius Jesus by Karl Jaspers
The Reappearance of the Christ and the Masters
of Wisdom by Benjamin Crème
The Wisdom Teachings of Archangel Michael by
Laura Jean Fleury
The Once and Future King
The Celestine Prophecy by James Redfi

Glossary

Saint Germain—the purported ascended master of freedom and the violet flame of transmutation; destined to reign with his twin flame Portia, the goddess of justice for the duration of the Aquarian cycle, also purported to be the sponsor of the United States of America.

Buddha—the purported lord of the world, succeeding Sunat Kumara in said office ca. 1985

Sanat Kumara—the purported higher arch of Venus, who then came to Terra to aid, said evolutions.

Maitreya—the purported cosmic Christ, second in office to that of Buddha, serving the evolutions of Terra and supposed leader of the Brotherhood of Masters.

Lucifer—an Archangel of the fire core or central sun, often mistakenly identified as the source of all evil, via some supposed rebellion against God, also viewed as the "tempter."

Paramahansa Yogananada—a 20ᵗʰ century Yogi or practitioner of the yogas, whose self-purported mission was to unite Christianity with the yoga's through a relocation to America to disseminate said beliefs.

Sri Yuketswar—the guru or teacher of Yogananda.

Morya—the ascended master of the blue ray serving God's will, commonly referred to as El Morya Khan in Elizabeth Clare Prophet disseminations.

Victory—a supposed ascended master hailing from Venus

John the Baptist—1st century Jewish prophet referenced as "El Baptismo."

Ra—a purported ancient alien social memory complex; disseminated a definite analytical system of "soul evolution" via dissemination through their "instrument."

Andrew Michael Lawless—self purported nut, hailing from Uranus, the Great Big Brown eye in the sky, a shithead, a turtle, a crowning, udderly tit-ilizingly insane, the Id.